CW00802475

1

James Egan was born in 1985 and grew up in
Portarlington, Co. Laois in the Midlands of Ireland.
In 2008, James moved to England and studied in Oxford.
James married his wife in 2012 and currently lives in
Havant in Hampshire.
James had his first book, 365 Ways to Stop Sabotaging
Your Life, published in 2014.
Several of James' books have become No.1 Best Sellers
in the UK including 1000 Facts about Horror Movies,
3000 Facts About the Greatest Movies Ever, 365 Things
People Believe That Aren't True, Another 365 Things
People Believe That Aren't True, and 500 Things People
Believe That Aren't True.

3000 Facts about Animals

(A compilation of 1000 Facts about Animals Vol. 1-3)

By

James Egan

Copyright 2016 © James Egan

All rights reserved. No part of this book may be reproduced,
stored, or transmitted by any means - whether auditory, graphic,
mechanical, or electronic - without written permission of both
publisher and author, except in the case of brief excerpts used in
critical articles and reviews. Unauthorized reproduction of any part
of this work is illegal and is punishable by law.

ISBN: 9781326723729

Because of the dynamic nature of the Internet, any web addresses
or links contained in this book may have changed since publication
and may no longer be valid. The views expressed in this work are
solely those of the author and do not necessarily reflect the views
of the publisher, and the publisher hereby disclaims any
responsibility for them.

Any people depicted in stock imagery provided by Thinkstock are
models, and such images are being used for illustrative purposes
only.

Lulu Publishing Services rev. date: 25/06/2016

Dedicated To

James "Yann" Lecheur

Content

Aardvarks

1. "Aardvark" means "earth pig."

2. This mammal is the only species in its order. Despite the fact it has a pig-like snout, kangaroo ears, an anteater-like tongue, and an opossum-tail, it's not related to any of these animals.

3. Aardvarks live south of the Sahara Desert.

4. Aardvarks are nocturnal.

5. Their spade-like claws allow them to dig through termite mounds to feast on the insects within. They can eat up to 50,000 insects in one night.

6. Their thick skin protects them from insect bites.

7. Their tongue is over 1ft long.

8. Its predators are hyenas, lions, leopards, and pythons.

9. When they escape from predators, they run in zig-zags.

10. Aardvarks will travel 20 miles to find food.

11. They have webbed feet, which allows them to swim with ease.

12. They create underground burrows with their claws. These holes usually have several entrances and can measure 13 meters long.

Alligators

13.   The easiest way to differentiate between an alligator and a crocodile is by observing their teeth. When an alligator closes its mouth, none of its teeth are visible. When a crocodile closes its mouth, some of its teeth stick out.

Alligators have wide, rounded snouts that are usually black. Crocodiles have narrow, pointed snouts that are normally grey-green.

14.   Alligators in Louisiana have learned to balance sticks on their snouts during heron-nesting season so birds will approach them to build nests. This is the only example of a predator using a lure based on seasonal prey behavior.

15.   Alligators go through up to 3,000 teeth in a lifetime. They have about 80 teeth at a time.

16.   Alligators can't take a single step backwards.

17.   They can weigh up to 1,000 lbs.

18.   Alligators can measure up to 11.2ft. The longest alligator ever was 19.2ft.

19.   They live for 50 years in the wild. In captivity, they can live for up to 80 years.

20.   Alligators were once on the verge of extinction. Thanks to strict conservation measures, this species is no longer endangered.

21.   Although the alligator has an incredibly strong bite, the muscles that open its mouth are very weak. A

child could easily hold an alligator's mouth shut and the reptile would be completely helpless.

22.   An alligator's gender is mainly based on temperature. Eggs that hatch in warm climate tend to become males and eggs that hatch in cold climate usually become females.

23.   Hitler had a pet alligator called Saturn. He lived until he was 85.

24.   Alligators can run slightly faster than humans.

25.   William Shakespeare invented the word "alligator." He derived the word from the Spanish "el lagarto," which means "the lizard."

<u>Alpacas</u>

26.   Their fleece is similar to sheep's wool except its thicker, less itchy, and flame-resistant.

27.   They can cross-breed with llamas. A crossbreed is called a huarizo. Huarizos have longer fleeces and are very desirable.

28.   Some alpaca-owners use this creature as a substitute for a lawnmower since it nibbles grass instead of pulling it out by the root.

29.   Alpacas need to be bought in pairs because they can die of loneliness.

30.   They were domesticated by the Incas 6,000 years ago.

31.   They come in 16 colors.

32.   A baby alpaca is called a cria.

Amphibians

33. An amphibian is any animal that is born with gills but eventually changes into a creature that breathes air.

34. There are three sub-categories of amphibians; frogs and toads, salamanders and newts, and caecilians.

35. Some amphibians don't have lungs. Instead, they breathe through their skin.

36. Amphibians are vertebrates (animals that have a spine.) Amphibians were the first vertebrates to live on land.

37. "Amphibian" means "two-lives."

38. There are at least 5,000 types of amphibians.

39. Amphibians are ectothermic (cold-blooded.)

40. The Meoposaurus algarvensis was a salamander the size of a small car that went extinct 200 million years ago. It was the largest amphibian to ever exist.

41. More than 75% of all frogs and toads live in tropical rainforests.

42. Caecilians are the least known type of amphibians. They don't have arms or legs and look like very long worms (about 4ft long.) They have a strong skull and a pointed nose.

43. Some amphibians have gills for their entire lives.

44. The worldwide amphibian population is on the decline.

45.   Batrachology is the study of amphibians.

46.   Herpetology is the study of amphibians and
        reptiles. The word, "herpetology" is derived from the
        Greek word, "herpien," which means "to creep."

47.   Because most amphibians breathe through their
        skin, amphibians are very sensitive to air pollution.

Ants

48.   Contrary to popular belief, ants aren't hard-working. In fact, they're really lazy. In any colony, 25% do absolutely no work, 77% do half of the work, and 3% never stop working.

49.   Ants cannot be seriously injured when they fall to the ground from a great height because their mass is evenly spread out in their body.

50.   They smell with their antennae.

51.   Fertile male ants are called drones.

52.   Their jaws open like scissors.

53.   Ants cannot swallow solid food. When they crush solid objects with their jaws, they drink the liquid within.

54.   Biologically, ants are most related to wasps.

55.   The worker ants protect their colony and their queen from predators.

56.   Some birds put ants in their feathers because their acids kill parasites.

57.   Each ant colony has a distinct smell, which allows each ant to recognize which colony other ants come from.

58.   Some ants never sleep.

59.   The Slave-Maker Ant steals pupae (baby ants) from other colonies and raises them as slaves.

60.   At night, worker ants move the eggs and larvae deep into the nest to keep them warm. During the daytime, the eggs and larvae are moved to the top of the nest so they are exposed to sunlight.

61.   A queen ant can live for over 10 years.

62.   Some male ants have wings.

63.   The queen licks the eggs to make them hatch.

64.   Some colonies can have three queens simultaneously.

65.   There are 12,000 ant species.

66.   The Bullet Ant is exactly what it sounds like; it's an ant that has a sting that is so painful, it feels like being shot.

67.   Most ants live for 45-60 days. However, the Pogonomyrmex Owyheei Ant is the longest living insect in the world and can live for 30 years.

68.   The jaws of a Trap-Jaw Ant are so strong, that the ants can use them to hurl its own bodies into the air to evade predators. Their jaws snap at 140mph, making them the fastest insects in the world.

69.   Some ants don't have eyes.

70.   Ants don't have ears. They rely on detecting vibrations in the ground so they know when a threat is near.

71.   Driver Ants were used to sew up wounds on soldiers

during World War I.

72.   A biologist that specializes in ants is called a myrmecologist.

73.   The Mycocepurus smithii Ant can clone itself. When a female ant learned how to duplicate itself, all of the male ants were kicked out of the colony and eventually died out. The all-female colony is now self-sustaining.

74.   Ants fight with each other all of the time. Myrmecologists say that when ants fight, they can hit each other with their antennae 20-42 times per second.

75.   Ant colonies have a designated area for going to the bathroom. Scientists find it odd that ants excrete waste inside the colony but throw dead ants outside.

76.   The Pheidole dentate is probably the weirdest kind of ant. Although they live for almost five months, their body doesn't seem to age in anyway until the last few days of its life. Studies have proved that these ants have no cell death in their brains and there is no decline of neurotransmitters like dopamine and serotonin at any point until days before death.

77.   There's 100 trillion ants on Earth. They weigh about the same as all of the humans in the world.

78.   The cordyceps is a parasitic fungus that can mind control ants and turn them into zombies, forcing them to spread the infection to others.

79.   The Hero Ant lives in cliffs and will latch onto intruding insects and then fling itself off the edge to its death, taking the intruder with them.

80. The Argentine Ant is the only animal on Earth apart from humans that has colonized three continents – Europe, South America and Asia.

81. A group of ants can create a bridge with their own bodies.

82. A team at the University of Lausanne in Switzerland learned that ants take riskier jobs as they get older.

83. Ants can be red, black, brown, yellow, green, or blue.

84. Carpenter ants mate while flying.

85. Worker ants are sterile.

86. The largest ant nest ever discovered measured 3,700 miles wide. It was found in Argentina in 2000. It was made up of over one billion ants.

87. An ant can carry 49 times its own body weight.

88. Ants are one of the few animals that can tell when they are sick and know how to medicate themselves. This concept is called zoophramacognosy. They usually medicate themselves by eating specific plants to flush out diseases.

Anteaters

89.   Anteaters lie in wait at the top of anthills and devour the ants that appear.

      However, anteaters know that if they destroy the hill, the ants will die. As a result, the anteater preserves the hill for future meals.

90.   An anteater can easily kill a human with its four-inch claws.

91.   They eat 70lbs worth of ants a day. That's about 35,000 ants every single day.

92.   Baby anteaters are called pups.

93.   Anteaters can eat up to 160 ants per minute.

94.   Their claws are curled under so they walk on their knuckles.

95.   Although most sources say that anteaters are carnivores, they also eat fruit that has fallen from trees.

96.   Three species of anteater can climb trees.

97.   Their extremely shaggy fur protects them from bites and stings.

98.   Anteaters have terrible vision and are almost deaf.

99.   Their body temperature is 32.7 degrees Celsius, which is very low for a mammal. By comparison, a human's body temperature is 37.1 degrees Celsius.

100.   Most anteaters live on their own.

101. Their tongue is 2ft long.

102. Aardvarks, numbats, echidnas, and pangolins are incorrectly identified as anteaters.

103. They are related to sloths and armadillos.

104. They are based in Central and South America.

105. An anteater's sense of smell is 40 times better than a human's.

106. A group of anteaters is called a parade.

107. They live for 15 years in the wild.

108. Anteaters are edentate (toothless) animals.

109. Some anteaters are the size of squirrels while others can measure 7ft in length.

Antelopes

110.   The difference between an antelope and a deer is that antelope have permanent antlers. Deer lose their antlers during certain seasons.

111.   There are 90 types of antelopes.

112.   An average-sized antelope weighs 1,300lbs.

113.   They normally live for 10 years.

114.   Antelopes can run 43mph.

115.   A group of antelopes is called a cluster, a herd, or a tribe.

116.   Most antelopes live in Africa but some species live in Asia and America.

117.   Antelopes have horizontal pupils.

118.   25 antelope species are endangered.

119.   Mountain goats aren't goats. They are antelopes.

120.   Antelope horns can grow up to 5ft long.

121.   Some antelopes have four horns instead of two.

122.   They communicate with each other through whistles, moos, trumpeting, and barks.

123.   The eland is the largest and slowest antelope. It can jump 8ft from a standstill.

124. The Royal antelope is the world's smallest antelope, measuring 10 inches tall. That's about the same size as a rabbit.

125. They usually follow zebras because antelopes know that zebras can easily locate grass.

126. Although most antelopes are herbivores, the duikers antelope eat bugs and birds.

127. The tauntaun creature in The Empire Strikes Back are based on the Saiga antelope.

128. Some antelopes stand on their hind legs to reach tree leaves.

<u>Apes</u>

129.   Apes are larger than monkeys and have a longer lifespan and a higher intelligence.
Also, monkeys have tails while apes do not.

130. The Gigantopithecus was a 10ft tall ape that lived thousands of years ago. It was the only ape that buried the dead.

131. Gorillas, chimpanzees, orangutans, and bonobos are in the category of the Great Apes.

132. Gibbons and siamangs are known as Lesser Apes.

133. A primatologist is someone who studies apes.

134. A group of apes is called a troop or a shrewdness.

135. A group of baboons is called a flange.

136. Ancient Egyptian police officers trained baboons to hunt criminals.

137. Apes feed off eggs, insects, birds, roots, barks, shrubs, leaves, and flowers.

138. The arms of an ape are longer than its legs.

139. Most animals rely on their smell or hearing.
However, apes rely on their vision just like humans.

140. Bonobo apes don't just mate for procreation. They mate to relieve tension in their group.

141. Female apes give birth every six or seven years.

142. Some apes can do mathematical puzzles faster than the average human.

143. Apes will blame other mistakes for their own mistakes.

144. The tarsier is only five inches tall, making it one of the smallest primates in the world. It's the only ape that communicates through ultrasound.

<u>Arachnids</u>

145.   There are 100,000 types of arachnids.

146.   Scorpions, spiders, tarantulas, ticks, mites, and daddy longlegs are arachnids.

147.   Arachnids have eight legs.

148.   Almost all arachnids are predators.

149.   Most arachnids have eight eyes. Some of them have 12 eyes while others have none.

150.   Most arachnids only eat liquid food. An arachnid injects a special goo into its prey that turns its insides into mush. The arachnid then sucks the liquefied innards into its own body.

151.   Arachnids have two main body parts; the cephalothorax and the abdomen.

152.   48,000 arachnid species are mites.

Badgers

153.   The earliest recorded use of the word "badger" was in 1523. Originally, badgers were known as brocks. The animal is referred to in Shakespeare's Twelfth Night but is called a brock. Its name is derived from the French word, "becheur," which means "digger."

154.   "Badger" used to mean "itinerant trader."

155.   A badger lives in an underground burrow called a sett.

156.   There are eight species of badger.

157.   They eat squirrels, mice, insects, vegetables, fruit, roots, groundhogs, rabbits, and snakes. They usually eat hundreds of earthworms every night.

158.   A badger can dig a hole in seconds, which is vital for staying alive while it is being chased by predators.

159.   A group of badgers is called a cette.

Bats

160. Of the 4,000 mammal species, over 1,100 of them are bats.

161. In the Bible, bats are referred to as birds.

162. Although bats have poor eyesight, there isn't one type of bat that is blind.

163. Bats use echolocation. This means that they call out to the environment and listen to the echoes to help them navigate and hunt.

164. Studying echolocation has drastically improved radars on submarines, ships, planes, spaceships, etc.

165. Echolocation is also known as sonar or bio-sonar.

166. Shrews, dolphins, rats, and whales also use echolocation.

167. Robert Galambos and Donald Griffin discovered that bats use echolocation in 1938.

168. Human beings can use echolocation. Some blind people make clicking sounds that will help them know what's around them based on the echoes that they sense.

169. Some bats screech through their nostrils.

170. Bats have been around for 50 million years.

171. The word "bat" means "good fortune" in China and Japan.

172.   The Bracken Bat Cave in Texas is made up of 20 million bats, making it the world's largest bat colony. When the bats leave the cave, radar systems thought it was a storm.

173.   Some bats can fly up to 250 miles in a single night.

174.   Although most bats are black or brown, some of them are orange or red.

175.   The anticoagulation agent in Vampire Bat spit is extremely effective against human stroke victims and people who have suffered heart attacks.

176.   Although the Dracula story originated in Eastern Europe, Vampire Bats only exist in Central and South America.

177.   Some bats have excellent eyesight. In fact, some are able to see ultraviolet light.

178.   The Pipistrelle Bat weighs less than two pennies and is as long as a human pinky finger. Despite its diminutive size, it eats 3,000 insects per night.

179.   A person who studies bats is called a chiropterologist.

180.   The Tube-Lipped Nectar Bat has the longest tongue of any mammal relative to body length. The tongue retracts into the bat's ribcage when it is not being used.

181.   Bat droppings are called guano. Guano is an extremely important fertilizer due to its high levels of phosphorus and nitrogen.

182. There are 45 kinds of bat in the US.

183. Although bats don't have a great reputation, there are the most efficient animals in the world at eating insects. According to Bat Conservation International, 150 Big Brown Bats can eat enough Cucumber Beetles in one summer to save farmers billions of dollars every year. If these bats didn't exist, Cucumber Beetles would produce up to 33 million larvae a year, which would destroy countless crops.

184. A bat's echolocation is so heightened, it can detect objects as thin as a human hair.

185. Humans can hear frequencies between 20 Hz and 20,000 Hz. Dogs can hear between 40 Hz and 60,000 Hz. However, bats can hear between 20 Hz and 120,000 Hz.

186. Only three bats drink blood.

187. Bats don't suck blood. Instead, they lap it.

188. During the US Civil War, bat droppings were used to make gunpowder.

189. White-Winged Vampire Bats snuggle up to hens and pretend to be chicks. When the birds are asleep, the bat feeds on their blood.

190. Bats mate and give birth while upside down.

191. Vikings called bats "ledrblaka," which means "leather flapper."

192. Vampire Bats have to drink their own weight in blood every day.

193.   Bats sleep upside down so they can fly away quickly if needed.

194.   Some bats eat frogs. They can tell which frogs are venomous by listening to their croaks.

195.   In bat colonies, all of the females have their babies at the same time.

196.   Vampire Bats rarely bite humans but if they do, they will try and find that same person the following night.

197.   Bats can tell people apart from their breath.

198.   During World War II, Americans tried to train bats to drop bombs.

199.   "Bat" means "hand wing."

200.   When bats were first seen, people thought they were flying mice.

201.   Originally, bats were called flutterers.

202.   Bats can fly two miles high.

203.   Bats can fly 60mph.

204.   Some bats live in spider webs.

205.   Small Club-Footed Bats roost inside bamboo stalks.

206.   A group of bats is called a cloud or a colony.

207. The Giant Golden-Crowned Flying Fox is the largest bat, with a wingspan of 1.8 meters.

208. Bats' legs are too thin to walk on.

209. Only one bat can't fly.

210. Bats are the only mammals that can fly.

211. 70% of bats eat insects. The rest eat fruit.

212. Vampire Bats are the only bats that can easily walk on the ground.

Bears

213.   There are eight species of bears – Sun Bear, Sloth Bear, Spectacled Bear, American Black Bear, Grizzly Bear, Polar Bear, Asiatic Black Bear, and the Giant Panda.

214.   Grizzly Bears can smell things up to 18 miles away.

215.   Bears are one of the few mammals that all of the same colors as a human.

216.   Bears have the best sense of smell in the world apart from elephants.

217.   A group of bears is called a sloth or a sleuth.

218.   A Grizzly Bear can crush a bowling ball with its teeth.

219.   Grizzly bears eat 20,000 calories a day.

220.   Male bears are called boars. Female bears are called sows.

221.   The Short-Faced Bear was the largest bear ever. In fact, it was the largest mammalian carnivore in history. It was 6.5ft while it was on all fours. It died out 12,000 years ago.

222.   The Sloth Bear has shaggier fur than any other bear.

223.   The Sun Bear has shorter fur than any other bear.

224.   You can tell the age of a bear by counting the rings inside of its tooth root.

225.   Bears have been known to roll rocks into bear traps to set them off so they can safely eat the bait inside.

226.   Bear live 30 years in the wild and 47 years in captivity.

227.   All bears (including the Giant Panda) are omnivores except the Polar Bear, which is a carnivore.

228.   Sun Bears have the longest claws of any bear.

229.   Sun Bears have the longest tongues of all bears, measuring 10 inches long.

230.   They can run up to 40mph. That's faster than a horse.

231.   Grizzly Bears have long, straight claws that allow them to dig.

232.   Black Bears have curved claws that allow them to climb trees.

233.   A bear's heartrate is 55 beats per minute. When it's hibernating, it's heartrate is nine beats per minute.

234.   Some bears can walk on their hind legs.

235.   Black Bears can be black, brown, red, or even white. When Native Americans first saw a Black Bear with white fur, they thought it was a ghost.

236.   Black Bears are the most common types of bears.

237. "Bear" means "bright brown."

238. Sun Bears are the smallest types of bears. They are the same size as a large dog.

239. Spectacled Bears are the only bears that live in South America.

240. The oldest known bear was the Dawn Bear. It lived 20 million years ago.

241. Bears have never lived in Australia or Antarctica. Although they don't live in Africa nowadays, bear fossils have been found there.

242. Bears have been known to eat snowmobiles, engine oil, and rubber.

243. Originally, lumber workers would kill bears that approached their buildings to avoid being attacked. Over time, they realized that it was easier and cheaper to bring food to the bears. Bears don't want to engage with humans and won't unless they are absolutely starving.

244. Bears have non-retractable claws.

245. Apart from Giant Pandas, all bears walk by putting their feet flat on the ground, just like humans. This type of walking is called "plantigrade." Most large animals like horses and elephants walk on their toes.

246. Apart from Giant Pandas and Polar Bears, bears are born without fur.

247. All bears are good swimmers.

248. The Ursa Major constellation is also known as the "Great Bear." It's the third largest constellation in the night sky.

249. Bears are the only large predators that regularly eat meat and plants.

250. Bears don't defecate during hibernation.

251. Ursinology is the study of bears.

252. The claws on their front feet are longer than the claws on their back feet.

253. Bears are related to coyotes.

254. Not all bears hibernate.

255. Baloo from The Jungle Book story is a Sloth Bear.

256. Their lips are not attached to their gums.

257. Thanks to Winnie the Pooh, many people believe bears like honey. Although it's true that bears attack bee hives, they prefer to eat bee larvae.

258. When Kodiak Brown Bears are born, they weigh 1lb. As an adult, they weigh 1,000lbs.

259. Lord Byron was told that he wasn't allowed to bring his pet dog to Cambridge, Oxford. Out of spite, he brought a bear since the school didn't have a rule that banned bears.

260. You are more likely to be killed by a teddy bear than a real bear.

Beavers

261. Beavers have transparent eyelids so they can see underwater when their eyes are shut.

262. Beavers are very sociable except when they are working.

263. Their teeth never stop growing.

264. They use their tails to steer, balance, and warn others.

265. They hiss when they are frightened.

266. Their bodies are designed in such a way, that they barely react to the cold. Although they can feel the cold, it will not deter them from working.

267. Their homes are made from trees and are called lodges. They indirectly create habitats for other species such as insects and birds when they form their lodges.

268. Beavers' dams cause and prevent floods.

269. Beavers cause up to $100 million in damages every year in the US.

270. The largest beaver damn is 850 meters in length. It is located in Wood Buffalo National Park, Canada. It is so vast, that it can be seen from space.

271. Beavers used to live in the UK but went extinct in the 1600s. They were reintroduced in Scotland in 2009.

272. A beaver can hold its breath for 15 minutes.

Bees

273. Bees can be trained to detect bombs.

274. The honey that humans eat has been puked out by bees.

275. Two spoonfuls of honey would be enough to fuel a bee to travel around the world.

276. A group of bees is usually called a swarm. However, they can also be called a cast, a cluster, a colony, a drift, an erst, a grist, a hive, a nest, a rabble, or a stand.

277. It is the only insect that produces food that is eaten by humans.

278. The honey that bees produce is the only food that contains pinocembrin, which is an antioxidant that improves brain functioning.

279. 33% of the food we eat depends on pollen. That means 1/3rd of all food exists because of bees.

280. 85% of bees live alone.

281. 20% of bees make honey.

282. A bee would have to visit two million flowers to produce a single pound of honey.

283. If you get stung by a bee, the best thing to use to remove the stinger is a credit card.

284. One colony of bees contains approximately 50,000 bees.

285. The queen bee will live for about five years.

286. Dumbledore isn't just the Headmaster of Hogwarts in the Harry Potter stories. The word "Dumbledore" is an old English term for the word "bumblebee."

287. The queen bee lays 2,500 eggs per day.

288. Drone bees mate but don't do any work. At winter, they are forced out of the hive.

289. Each colony has a unique odor.

290. Worker bees are all female.

291. Bees pollinate flowers, which is responsible for 70% of all fruit, vegetables, nuts, and seeds on Earth.

292. Bees have two stomachs; one for eating and one for storing nectar.

293. Bees have five eyes; two compound eyes and three tiny ocelli eyes.

294. Bees have existed for 30 million years.

295. The average worker bee makes 8% of a teaspoon of honey in her entire life.

296. A single beehive makes about 100lbs of honey. Beekeepers only harvest the excess honey. They can't take anymore or all of the bees in the hive would die.

297. Although the queen bee has a stinger, she won't use it since she never leaves the hive.

298. Only worker bees sting.

299. Bee venom is used to fight the AIDS virus.

300. Bees fly at 16mph.

301. According to scientists, the most painful place to be stung by a bee is the inside of the nose. They figured this out the hard way.

302. Flowers use electric fields to attract pollinating insects. Bees detect this energy with the tiny hairs on their bodies; buzzing near a set of flower sets off something like a static charge, which bends the hair and directs them to flowers nearby.

303. Bees are assigned jobs depending on their age.

304. When a bee is 1-2 days old, it spends its time cleaning cells, starting with the ones it was born in. When a bee is 3-5 days old, they feed older larvae. When they are 6-11 days old, they feed the youngest larvae. When they are 12-17 days old, they produce wax, build combs, carry food, and perform undertaker duties. When they are 18-21 days old, they guard the hive. When they are 22 days old or older, they collect pollen, nectar, and water.

305. Bees live for about 45 days.

306. They can fly for up to six miles at a time.

307. A honey bee's wings move 230 beats per second. The rapid speed of their wings is what creates the buzzing associated with bees.

308. A hive of bees will fly 90,000 miles to collect 2lbs of honey.

309. Bees instinctively know that the world is round.

310. Bees dance to communicate where to find food.

311. Bees are able to find the shortest route through multiple locations better than any animal in the world.

312. When bees were given cocaine, they would exaggerate to other bees on the quality of food they found. That's right. Scientists give bees cocaine for some reason.

313. Bees can smell flowers a hundred times better than humans.

314. They can see in ultraviolet light.

315. Bees can become drastically different depending on what queen they have.

316. Bees don't always die when they sting.

317. Bees are cold-blooded.

318. Genetically, bees are related to ants.

319. A honeybee's sense of smell is better than any dog.

320. A bee visits 50-100 flowers during a collection trip.

321. The bee's brain is oval shaped and is the size of a sesame seed.

322. When the queen bee is too old to rule the hive, the worker bees cluster around her until she dies from overheating. This process is known as "cuddle death."

Beetles

323. A beetle is an insect with a plated exoskeleton and hard forewings called elytra.

324. Beetles are endopterygotes, which means they undergo complete metamorphosis, where their entire body changes throughout their life.

325. The Dung Beetle is the world's strongest animal. It can pull an object 1,141 times its own weight.

326. The biological term for a beetle is coleopteran, which means "sheathed wing."

327. Beetles are the most varied subspecies in the world. They make up 25% of all known life-forms.

328. 40% of insects are beetles.

329. There are approximately 300,000 species of beetles that have yet to be classified.

330. The longest beetle is Titanus giganteus, which measures 6.8 inches.

331.   Dermestid Beetles are used in museums to clean the bones of exhibits.

332. When fighting predators, the Bombardier Beetle will mix chemicals in its body, turning itself into a living bomb. When it explodes, it spews acid in all directions.

333. The Fringe Ant Beetle is the smallest of its kind, measuring 0.25mm.

334. The Goliath Beetle is the largest of its kind,

measuring 4.3 inches and weighing 100g.

335. Beetles have existed for 270 million years.

336. The Ladybird was called Our Lady's Bird by Catholics and was seen as the intercessor between mankind and the Virgin Mary. The red on the insect signified the blood of Christ and the seven spots on its back represented the seven sorrows of Mary.

337. The Ancient Egyptians worshipped a beetle god called Kepri. They believed he rolled the Sun up the hill every morning, much like how a Dung Beetle rolls a ball of dung.

338. The Beatles came up with the name of their band because they liked insects but they wanted a name that reflected beat music.

Birds

339.   A bird is a warm-blooded vertebrate characterized by feathers, toothless beaked jaws, fused collarbones, and the laying of hard-shelled eggs.

340.   There are 9,865 species of bird.

341.   When a bird is born, it is covered in a material called down. Down is an insulating padding that looks like foam. As the hatchling gets older, the down falls out and is replaced with feathers.

342.   1,227 bird species are on the verge of extinction.

343.   133 bird species have gone extinct since 1500.

344.   The kiwi is the only bird with nostrils at the end of its bill.

345.   The kakapo bird is so critically endangered that there was a time where there were only two left on the entire planet.

346.   Feathers help birds fly and provide waterproofing and insulation. They also block harmful UV rays from reaching the bird's skin.

347.   Up to 3.7 billion birds are killed by cats every year in the US.

348.   Most birds look like their knees bend backwards. This "knee" is actually the bird's ankle.

349.   Birds instinctively latch onto branches while they sleep. Because they do this with their tendons instead of their muscles, the bird can sleep without falling off.

350.   Male songbirds can sing up to 2,000 times a day.

351.   Songbirds baby-talk to their young. They sing shorter and more repetitive tunes to teach their chicks.

352.   A human can eat effortlessly even if he or she is upside down. However, birds need gravity to swallow their food. Because of this, birds cannot be taken onto spaceships since the lack of gravity would mean they would choke to death when they ate.

353.   The oldest bird is the Archaeopteryx, which lived 140 million years ago. This black bird was the size of a chicken. Although it could fly, it could run and climb trees.
        Some paleontologists suggest there was an earlier bird called the Protoavis that existed 220 million years ago but results have proved inconclusive.

354.   The largest flying bird was the Argentavis. This creature lived five million years ago. Its wingspan was seven meters and it weighed as much as a gorilla.

355.   There are 40 species of flightless birds.

356.   Avocados are poisonous to birds.

357.   Since nicotine wards off parasites, city birds line their nests with cigarette butts.

358.   Birds have evolved to be as light as possible in order for them to fly. As a result, they have incredibly light skeletons. In fact, the feathers of a bird weigh more than its skeleton.

359.   Human lungs take up 5% of space in the body. Bird lungs take up 20% of body space.

360.   There are 40 million pet birds in the US.

361.   The largest bird of prey is the Andean condor, weighing 27lbs.

362.   The most common wild bird is the Red-Billed Quelea. There's at least three million in Africa.

363.   There is a myth that if you touch a bird's nest, the mother bird will abandon its eggs. There is no science to back this up.

364.   Arctic Terns have the longest annual migration of any bird. They travel from the Arctic to the Antarctic and then back again.

365.   66% of bird species are found in tropical rain forests.

366.   The European Wren can sing 700 notes in less than a minute and can be heard from 500 meters away.

367.   The male Lyrebird can mimic the calls of over 20 birds. It can also perfectly imitate the sound of a camera, a chainsaw, or a car alarm.

368.   The kiwi lays the largest egg proportioned to its size. Its egg is 25% the size of an adult kiwi.

369.   The bigger a bird is, the longer it takes for its egg to hatch. The eggs of small birds can hatch in two weeks. The eggs of large birds can take two months to hatch.

370.   The most dangerous bird to humans is the cassowary. It can kill a human with one kick.

371.   Birds have evolved so they don't lose much heat when they walk on ice.

372.   While directing the horror film, The Birds, Alfred Hitchcock would feed the birds whiskey to stop them from flying away.

373.   Birds eat 20% of their body weight to receive the energy needed to fly.

374.   Birds can see ultraviolet light. As a result, they can see electric energy spewing out of power lines, and so will avoid them.

375.   The King of Saxony Bird-of-Paradise (that is its scientific name) has eyebrows that are larger than its entire body.
        They serve no purpose. Except to look cool.

376.   The Large Wandering Albatross lives for 80 years, which is longer than any other bird. It also has the longest wingspan, measuring 11.8ft. It can soar for six hours without moving its wings.

377.   For the first five or six years of its life, the albatross will usually not touch the ground once. They will either be in the air or the sea.

378.   The scientific term for a bird of prey is a raptor.

379. Have you ever wondered what the difference is between an eagle, a falcon, and a hawk? They are very similar since they are all birds of prey. Although the eagle and hawk are in the same bird family

(Accipitridae,) falcons are of a different family called Falconidae.

Eagles are the largest of the three, measuring about 2ft with a wingspan of up to two meters.

Hawks are only 1ft in size.

Falcons are the smallest, measuring only 25cm.

Falcons are best known for their speed. Falcons are far faster than eagles and hawks.

Buffalos

380. Many people get buffalo and bison mixed up.
Although they are part of the Bovidae family, they have
many differences.

Bison have shaggy coats. Buffalo have short, glossy
coats. Buffalos have much larger horns and have been
domesticated. Bison live in North America and buffalo
live in Asia and Africa.

People get them mixed up because they are about the
same size. They stand 6ft tall, 10ft long, and weigh a ton.

381. A group of buffalo is called an obstinacy.

382. Buffalos are four times stronger than oxen.

383. They have been known to kill lions.

384. Another animal that gets mixed up with the buffalo is
the wisent. A wisent is genetically linked to the bison.
It's also known as the wood bison.

385. Despite its name, the American buffalo is a bison, not
a buffalo. What makes this more confusing is that it has
short horns so it looks like a buffalo.

386. A herd is usually composed of 12 buffalo.

387. Buffalo have exceptional memories. There have been
many cases where a buffalo will recognize a hunter that
shot at it years ago and will immediately attack him.

388. They normally live for 20 years.

<u>Bugs</u>

389. The biological term for a bug is a Hemiptera.

390. A bug is an insect with a sucking mouthpart.

391. Common bugs include cicadas, aphids, planthoppers, leafhoppers, and shield bugs.

392. Some insects have "bug" in their name even though they are not classified as such. A ladybug is a beetle and the lovebug is a fly.

393. There are up to 80,000 bug species.

394. The first computer bug was caused by an actual bug in 1947.

395. The Ant-Killing Assassin Bug liquidates ants with an enzyme. It then uses their carcasses as a camouflaging body-armor.

Butterflies

396. Butterflies like drinking blood.

397. Amazonian butterflies drink turtle tears.

398. There's a butterfly called 89'98 because the markings on its wings look like the numbers, 89 and 98.

399. Butterflies taste with their feet.

400. Female butterflies are large than males, which is rare in the animal kingdom.

401. Some butterflies pollinate flowers.

402. They can't fly if they are cold.

403. They smell with their antennae.

404. Most butterflies live for a month. Some live for three days while others live for 10 months.

405. Butterflies don't eat; they only drink.

406. They can only see the colors, red, green, and yellow.

407. Butterflies don't grow in size.

408. The Queen Alexandria's Birdwing is the largest butterfly and has a wingspan of 11 inches.

409. A group of butterflies is called a flutter.

410. There are 20,000 species of butterfly.

Camels

411. Camels hold grudges and wait months to exact their revenge.

412. Baby camels are born without humps.

413. Baby camels bleat like a lamb.

414. A camel's hump stores fat, not water.

415. Asian camels have two humps. Arabian camels have one.

416. Surprisingly, Australia has more camels than any other country.

417. A camel can drink 135 liters in 15 minutes.

418. A group of camels is called a caravan.

419. There are 160 words for camel in the Arabic language.

420. They are vegetarians.

421. There are 17 million camels worldwide.

422. Their milk is lower in fat and sugar than cow's milk.

423. 90% of camels have one hump.

424. They have a double row of long, curly eyelashes to keep out sand and dust.

425. They can easily kick with all four of their legs, which is rare for a quadrupedal (four-footed) animal.

426. Unlike most mammals, camels have oval-shaped red cells, not circular ones. This ensures the blood flows when the camel is in a dehydrated condition.

427. They are good swimmers.

428. A human's body temperature is 37.1 degrees Celsius. A camel's body temperature is 41 degrees Celsius.

429. Their lips are so thick, they can easily eat thorny plants.

430. In Arab cultures, camels represent patience, tolerance, and endurance.

431. Camels have three eyelids.

432. They can live for up to 50 years.

433. Camel humps are about 30 inches long.

434. Camels can survive without drinking for almost three months.

435. They can carry 500lbs on their backs.

436. Camels are usually 6ft high and 10ft long. They can weigh from 1,320-2,200lbs.

Cats

437.   Ancient Egyptians worshipped the cat-god, Bast and held felines in high regard. If a cat died in Ancient Egypt, every member of the household would shave their eyebrows off in mourning. If an Ancient Egyptian killed a cat, even by accident, they would receive the death penalty.

438.   Cats have three blood types.

439.   A group of cats can be called a pounce, a glaring, a clutter, or a clowder.

440.   The rarest cat in the world is the Bornean Bay Cat. Only 12 of them have been recorded between 1874 and 2002. It was only spotted on film in 2009.

441.   In the 1960s, two Siamese cats kept meowing and clawing at the walls of the Holland embassy in Moscow. Their owners investigated, assuming that the cats had found mice. Instead, they found microphones hidden by Russian spies.

442.   There are 88 million cats in the US, making them the country's most popular pet.

443.   Cats use 32 muscles to control their outer ear. Humans only have six muscles in their ear.

444. The average cat has 26 whiskers.

445.   There are over 70 cat breeds.

446.   Cats can hear ultrasound.

447.   Cats have a "righting reflex" that allows them to survive enormous falls. There have been reports of cats surviving from over 43 stories.

448.   Cats sweat through their paws.

449.   The CIA spent $20 million the 1960s to train cats to spy on the Soviets. The first spy cat was hit by a taxi.

450.   Neutered cats live 62% longer than unneutered ones.

451.   Cats can make over 100 distinctive sounds. Dogs can only make 10.

452.   Cats have unique noseprints like the way humans have fingerprints.

453.   A cat called Dusty produced 420 kittens in her life, which is the world record.

454.   The first cat in space was called Felicette.

455.   The most effective way to tell if an earthquake is imminent is to see how many cats have gone missing. If the number has trebled, an earthquake is on the way.

456.   Cats have killed off at least 33 different animals, making them responsible for more animal extinctions than any other creature apart from humans.

457.   Cats are incapable of feeling forgiveness.

458.   Cats injured 40,000 US citizens every year.

459.   A cat's tail contains nearly 10% of all of the bones in its body.

460. Cats can become so addicted to tuna, that they will refuse to eat anything else.

461. The Sand Cat is the only feline that lives in the desert.

462. Sand Cats rarely get attacked because they always look like kittens.

463. Cats are left-pawed or right-pawed like the way humans are left-handed or right-handed.

464. The parasite, Toxoplasma gondii, can only breed inside the guts of cats. When it infects rats, the microscopic organism alters the rodents' behavior so they become less scared of cats.

465. Cats can't taste sweet things.

466. If a cat goes missing in the US, there's a 75% chance he or she will return safely.

467. The longest cat ever was 4ft long.

468. If a cat urinates on your belongings, it's because it's marking it with its scent to warn predators that its protecting you. If this happens, don't lash out at the cat. If you do, it will feel like you don't appreciate its "kind gesture," which means it's more likely to misbehave in the future.

469. Although cats love milk, they shouldn't drink it as it makes their teeth fall out.

470. A cat's kidneys are so advanced, that they can survive on seawater.

471. A cat will present its belly to its owner as a sign of trust. When a cat does this, most people think it wants to play. To the cat, it's more like a hug.

472. The oldest video of cats was made in 1894 by Thomas Edison. The video shows two cats wearing boxing gloves fighting in a boxing ring.

473. Most people think that cats look so cute when they lick themselves, that they stroke them as a sign of affection. Cats HATE when people do this because they just covered the cat's body with the human's scent, so they have to clean themselves again!

474. When a cat is confronted with a predator, it will arch its back and hiss. This is a sign of fear, not anger. It's a bluff because the cat doesn't want to fight.

475. Telling a cat that you love it means nothing. The best way to show affection to a cat is to stare at it for a few seconds and then blink very slowly. The cat will usually do the same thing as a sign of trust.

476. A cat sleeps for 66% of its life.

477. When cats chase their prey, they keep their head level. Dogs and humans bob their head when they are running.

478. The technical term for a cat's hairball is a bezoar.

479. A cat's brain is more similar to a human's than a dog's.

480. There are 500 million domestic cats worldwide.

481. The website, Buzzfeed, has posted over 22,500 articles about cats since 2006. In my opinion, this is still not enough.

482. During the Spanish Inquisition, Pope Innocent VIII condemned cats as evil and had thousands of them burned to death. With so many cats dead, the population of rats exploded, which exasperated the effects of the Black Death, which lead to the demise of 33% of Europeans.

483. Cats can easily climb trees but they have no idea how to get down? But why is this?
    Well, every cat's paws point the same way. To get down a tree, a cat must climb backwards, which is counter-intuitive to their nature.

484. According to Hebrew legend, Noah prayed to God for help so the rats on the Ark wouldn't eat the stored food. In reply, God made a lion sneeze and a cat popped out. It doesn't actually say this in the Bible since cats are never mentioned once in the entire book.

485. Although dogs have a better sense of smell than a cat, cats have superior hearing. Cats can hear two octaves higher than a human.

486. Cats can detect cancer in humans, especially breast cancer.

487. Cats can run 31mph.

488. 300,000 mummified cats have been found in Ancient Egypt.

489. Most cats give birth to 1-9 kittens.

490. The largest cat litter was made up of 19 kittens. 15 survived.

491. A cat can leap five times its own height in a single bound.

492. Many Siamese cats are cross-eyed.

493. In the original story of Cinderella, the fairy godmother was a cat.

494. The Egyptian Mau is the oldest breed of cat.

495. Someone who loves cats is called an ailurophile.

496. Cat owners are 30% less likely to suffer a heart attack.

497. There are many reports of cats travelling hundreds or even thousands of miles to their home after they get lost. Cats accomplish this using "psi-travelling." Experts believe cats use the angle of the sunlight to find their way home or they have magnetized cells in their brains that act as a compass.

498. Isaac Newton invented the cat flap.

499. Grass appears red to cats.

500. A female cat is called a molly.

501. Cats don't like water because their fur doesn't insulate well when it's wet.

502. Cats evolved from a carnivore called the proailus 25 million years ago. Hyenas and mongooses also originated from this creature.

503. The Turkish Van might be the only cat that likes swimming.

504. A cat's jaw can't move sideways, so it can't chew large portions of food.

505. Cats rarely meow to other cats.

506. Cats don't purr because they are happy. They purr to vibrate their skeleton, which prevents bone-related illnesses like arthritis. The reason why cats purr when you stroke them is because you are adjusting its posture and it's trying to re-align it.

507. The more kittens sleep, the larger they will become when they are adults.

508. The heaviest cat ever was Tabby, who weighed 47lbs.

509. The oldest cat ever was 38. Since an average cat lives for 15 years, this would be like a human being living to 200.

510. The first Cat Show took place in 1871 in London.

511. Felix the Cat was the first cartoon cat in 1919.

512. Cats should never eat onions, garlic, potatoes, chocolate, grapes, raisins, or tomatoes.

513. A cat's heartrate is 140 beats per minute. By comparison, a human's is 72 beats per minute.

514. The largest domestic cat is the Ragdoll, which weighs 20lbs.

515. There are 60 million feral cats in the US.

516. Since cats have no collarbone, they can fit through any opening larger than their head.

517. When Abraham Lincoln's wife was asked what her husband's hobbies were, she said, "Cats."

518. In the Austin Powers movies, Dr. Evil has a cat called Mr. Bigglesworth. The cat's real name is SGC Belfry Ted Nude-Gent.

519. 0.5% of cats are allergic to humans. Being exposed to humans will trigger asthma in the feline.

520. When a cat realizes it is fatally ill, it will find a quiet spot away from their owner to die in peace. A cat does this because it knows its body will attract predators and it doesn't want them to be near its owner. Although cats are known for being selfish animals, their last act in life is completely altruistic.

Caterpillars

521. Caterpillars have no purpose except to eat enough to sustain themselves to adulthood when they become a butterfly or a moth.

522. When it reaches maturity, the caterpillars melt down into a sac of fluid, which then creates the entire butterfly or moth from scratch.

523. A caterpillar can consume 27,000 times its body weight during its lifetime.

524. The first thing a caterpillar eats is its own eggshell.

525. Caterpillars have 12 eyes called stemmata.

526. Despite how small a caterpillar is, it has 4,000 muscles.

527. Despite what a caterpillar looks like, it only has six legs. The other appendages are prolegs and are designed to hold onto plants or climb, not to walk.

528. There are 180,000 types of caterpillar

529. Caterpillars live for about three weeks.

530. The Lonomia Obliqua is known as the Killer Caterpillar (I call it the Caterkiller.) It's almost as venomous as a rattle snake and has killed over 500 people since 1967.

Chameleons

531.   The chameleon is known for changing colors. However, it does this to express how it feels, not to camouflage.

532.   There are 160 species of chameleon.

533.   They can be found in Hawaii, California, Florida, southern Europe, Africa, south Asia, and Sri Lanka.

534.   59 species live on the island of Madagascar.

535.   It takes about 20 seconds for a chameleon to change color.

536.   The cells that make the chameleon change colors are called chromatophores.

537.   They can look in two different locations at once.

538.   The smallest chameleon is the Brookesia micra. It measures 15mm and can easily stand on a human fingernail.

539.   The largest chameleon is the Furcifer oustaleti, measuring 2.3ft.

540.   The chameleon projects its tongue at great speed to latch onto prey. This is known as a ballistic tongue. The tip of its tongue has a stick bulbous muscle, which works like a suction cup. This prevents the prey from escaping.

541.   Its tongue can be twice the length of the chameleon.

542.   It can project its tongue in 0.07 seconds.

543.   They rely on hearing sound frequencies rather than direct sound.

544.   They have ultraviolet vision.

545.   The male is more ornamented and usually has spikes and horns on their heads, spine, and tail.

Cheetahs

546. Cheetahs are the fastest land animals in the world. They can accelerate from 0 to 60mph in three seconds. It can run up to 75mph for a few seconds. When a cheetah is moving at a maximum speed of 60mph, it is in the air more than on the ground.

547. Their name is derived from the Hindu word "chita," which means "spotted one."

548. It's genus name is Acinonyx, which means "no move claw" in Greek. The name refers to the fact that the cheetah is the only big cat that can't sheath its claws.

549. Cheetahs are the only cat that are designed for running, not leaping.

550. Unlike most big cats, cheetahs have poor night vision and aren't very good at climbing trees.

551. Cheetahs only need to drink every four days.

552. Only 10,000 exist in the wild in Africa.

553. They can weigh up to 150lbs.

554. They eat antelope, zebra, hares, and rodents.

555. Its prey are baboons, hyenas, and lions.

556. 90% of cheetahs die before they reach adulthood.

557. Baby cheetahs have a white streak on their back, which makes them look like a honey badger. Since honey badgers are the most ferocious animals on Earth, predators like lions and hyenas will leave baby cheetahs

alone.

558.   Cheetahs, tigers, jaguars, and other wild cats are attracted to the Calvin Klein's "Obsession" scent.

Chickens

559.   Chickens have 266% more fat than they did 40 years ago.

560.   700ft is the greatest height that a chicken egg has been dropped without cracking.

561.   A chicken was discovered in Japan that had tail feathers that measured 34.7ft.

562.   There's a rare breed of chicken that has black meat, skin, organs, bones, bone marrow, tongue, and eyes. You can buy one for $2,500.

563.   The dangly bit below a rooster's beak is called a wattle.

564.   A chicken can lay 300 eggs a year.

565.   A group of chickens is called a flock or a brood.

566.   A group of chicks is called a peep.

567.   A group of chicken eggs is called a clutch.

568.   Chickens make 30 different vocalizations to communicate.

569.   Bird flu will kill at least 90% of a flock of chickens within 48 hours.

570.   A mother hen can turn her eggs up to 50 times a day.

571.   The largest chicken egg ever weighed 12oz.

572.   There is misconception that chickens and turkeys can breed to form turkens. This isn't true.

573.   The most eggs every laid by one chicken in 24 hours is seven.

574.   A chicken with red ear lobes will produce brown eggs. A chicken with white ear lobes will produce white eggs. In terms of nutrition or taste, there is no difference between a white egg and a brown egg.

575.   The chicken was the first bird to have its genome sequenced in 2004 in order to better understand DNA.

576.   The chicken is the animal that is most related to the Tyrannosaurus Rex. In fact, a paleontologist called Jack Horner (that's his real name) believes we can recreate dinosaurs by combining chicken DNA with dinosaur DNA. If it is successful, he wishes to call the dinosaur the chickenosaurus.

577.   The oldest chicken ever was 22.

578.   Chickens dream.

579.   Many people eat egg whites, believing they are filled with protein while the yolk contains all of the fat. This isn't true. Both pieces of the egg have protein and fat.

580.   Chickens can't taste anything sweet or salty.

581.   A chicken can become so stressed, its feathers can fall out.

582.   The most yolks to ever form in one egg is nine.

583.   Very rarely, a second eggshell can form within an egg.

584.   In Gainesville, Georgia, it's illegal to eat fried chicken with anything except your fingers.

585.   There are 25 billion chickens in the world, which is more than any other bird species.

586.   Chickens were domesticated in 6000B.C. for cockfights, not food.

587.   The longest a chicken has ever flown for was 13 seconds.

588.   Chickens eat insects, mice, and even lizards.

589.   There 12 types of chickens such as the Dutch Bantam, the Leghorn, and the Rhode Island Red.

590.   When a chicken dances, it's called tidbitting.

591.   A baby female chick is called a pullet.

592.   Chickens have more bones in their neck than giraffes.

593.   Anyone who has been taught basic science knows that there are three basic states of matter – solid, liquid, and gas. As science has progressed, 13 more states of matter have been discovered.
        In 2014, a new state of matter was discovered... inside the eyeball of a chicken! This crystallized liquid is called disordered uniformity.

Chimpanzees

594. Humans have more hair than chimpanzees. Chimps appear to have more hair than humans because their hair is thicker.

595. There can be 15-120 chimps in a chimpanzee community.

596. They usually travel in groups of six.

597. There are about 150,000 chimps in the wild.

598. They live in 21 African countries.

599. Mother chimps give birth to one youngling ever five or six years.

600. Young chimps stay with their mothers until they are about 10 years old.

601. Mother chimps are pregnant for eight months.

602. Their only predator is the leopard.

603. Michael Jackson and Elvis Presley had pet chimps.

604. They live for 50 years.

605. They can stand as tall as 4.5ft.

606. They can weigh 55-110lbs.

607. Like gorillas, chimps can catch and spread human diseases like measles, ringworm, hepatitis B, and the flu.

608. They can be taught sign language and learn up to 240

words.

609. Chimps can recognize each other from their call.
Their call is known as a pant-hoot.

610. Chimps groom each other when they get stressed.

611. Chimps show affection by kissing, patting others on
the back, holding hands, and tickling.

612. When they are sick, they eat medical plants to heal
themselves.

613. Baby chimps have a white tail tuft that disappears as
they grow older.

614. Like humans, chimps have opposable thumbs. Unlike
humans, they have opposable big toes.

615. Chimps are one of the smartest animals on Earth.

616. They use large sticks as clubs and throw them at
leopards.

617. The male chimp is called a blackback. A female chimp
is called an empress.

618. Despite their small size, a chimp is six times stronger
than an adult male human.

619. Chimps are omnivores. They eat bark, stems, roots,
flowers, leaves, and seeds. They eat the meat of goats,
antelopes, baboons, and monkeys.

620. 98.4% of chimpanzee DNA is identical to human
DNA.

Classes

621.   Most people know of animal classes such as mammals, fish, birds, reptiles, insects, etc. However, there were other animal classes throughout history that no longer exist. One of the oddest animal classes was the graptolites; marine superorganisms comprised of many microscopic animals. They were all connected to each other via a nerve cord. This animal class went extinct 315 million years ago.

622.   An animal class can also be known as a biological family or clade.

623.   An annelid class includes most worms including earthworms, ringworms, tapeworms, and leeches.

624.   There are 17,000 types of annelids.

625.   Helicoplacoids are an extinct animal class that evolved into animals like starfish and sea cucumbers (which are classed as echinoderms.) Helicoplacoids were about two inches large and resembled tiny armored footballs. They lived in mud and fed off plankton.

626.   Halwaxiids are an extinct animal class that evolved into mollusks. They looked like scaly worms or feathered pinecones. They measured about two inches long.

627.   Conodonts were like fish except they didn't have backbones. These three-inch creatures died out 200 million years ago.

628.   Synapsids were reptile-mammal hybrids that existed 300 million years ago.

Cockroaches

629.   The most common cockroach in Europe is the Ectobius.

630.   A cockroach can live for weeks without its head but will eventually die from starvation.

631.   Cockroaches that have been raised on a spaceship become quicker, stronger, and tougher than Earth cockroaches.

632.   Cockroaches shed their skin.

633.   Cockroaches existed 120 million years before dinosaurs.

634.   Cockroaches can't stand catnip.

635.   Cockroaches can run on two legs.

636.   A group of cockroaches is called an intrusion.

637.   A baby cockroach is called a nymph.

638.   Cockroaches can run 5ft per second, which is very impressive for an insect.

639.   Fried cockroaches are a common meal in Thailand and China.

640.   Cockroaches are 15 times more resistant to radiation than humans.

641.   Surgeons have performed brain surgery on cockroaches.

Cows

642. Cows sleep for about three hours per day.

643. Despite what many sources say, cows do not have four stomachs. They have one stomach with four chambers – the rumen, reticulum, omasum, and abomasum.

644. Cows always face north or south while eating. Nobody knows why and nobody knows how they can tell.

645. Cows moo in accents.

646. Cow DNA is 80% identical to human DNA.

647. When a matador shakes a red cape at a bull, the animal gets angry and charges towards him. However, the bull gets angry because of the motion of the cape, not the red color. Bulls can't see the red or green.

648. Cows moo. Bulls bellow. Calves bawl.

649. If a cow and a yak mate, they will have a dzo. These animals are popular in Mongolia.

650. If a cow and a buffalo mate, they will have a beefalo. A beefalo looks like an extremely fluffy cow.

651. 60 cows will produce one ton of milk per day.

652. You can tell the age of a bull by counting the rings in its horns.

653. Cows eat 40lbs of food per day.

654. Cows eat the equivalent of a bathtub full of water on a daily basis.

655. Cows live for about 20 years.

656. Cows can sleep standing up. However, they only dream if they sleep while lying down.

657. They can run up to 20mph.

658. A bull can weigh up to 2,425lbs.

659. There are 800 breeds of cow.

660. The skin of 3,000 cows are needed for a year's supply of footballs for the NFL.

661. One burger from a fast food restaurant is made up of about 100 cows.

662. Cows have 800 blood types.

Crabs

663. Crabs have 10 limbs; eight normal legs and two giant claws.

664. The Japanese Spider Crab is the largest crab in the world, measuring 13ft across.

665. Crabs can live for over a century.

666. There are two types of crabs; true crabs (brachyurans) and false crabs (anomurans.) True crabs have a short abdomen and use four pairs of long legs for walking. These include Blue Crabs, Spider Crabs, and Ghost Crabs. False crabs have long abdomens and fewer walking legs. They include Hermit Crabs and King Crabs.

667. There are 5,000 types of crabs. 4,500 of them are true crabs.

668. They can use their front claws as a vice for crushing or like a scissors for cutting. They can also use them like chopsticks to pick up food.

669. The Sally Lightfoot is the brightest crab in the world. It's red, orange, yellow, and white.

670. They can be found in the ocean, near volcanos, in trees, on land, and even under the ice in Antarctica.

671. The word "cancer," is derived from the word "crab" in Latin. Greek physicians, Hippocrates and Galen, believed tumors looked like crabs.

672. Male crabs have a triangular abdomen while female crabs have a rounder one.

673. 20% of all animals that humans catch in the sea are crabs.

674. Genetically, crabs are related to spiders.

675. The Horse Crab is the most consumed crab in the world.

676. The Pea Crab is the smallest crab. Unsurprisingly, it is the size of a pea.

677. When a crab is born, it is the size of a grain of salt.

678. Female crabs lay millions of eggs at once.

679. A group of crabs is called a cast.

680. Humans eat 1.5 million tons of crab a year.

681. They usually lose a leg or a claw in a fight. Over time, it will grow back.

682. A crab's shell doesn't stretch. When a crab gets bigger, it must climb out of its shell and grow a new one.

683. Crabs have teeth in their stomachs, not their mouths.

684. Crabs molt once or twice per year.

685. They can live on land as long as they keep their gills moist.

686. A male crab is called a jimmy. A female crab is called a jenny.

687. Fiddler crabs have one large claw, which they use to

impress mates and intimidate predators.

688. If you put a group of crabs in a bucket, very few of them will escape. When a crab gets near the edge, another crab will drag it back because it wants to escape first. If each crab allowed the other crabs to escape, they would all get out of the bucket within minutes. But because they don't help each other, it can take hours before a single crab frees itself from the bucket. This is known as the "Crab Mentality" or "Crabs in a Barrel."

This concept has been used as a metaphor for people's goals. Any time a person wants to accomplish something, people will make fun of them for it because they are jealous that they themselves aren't doing anything productive with their life. It's a mentality that boils down to "If I can't have what I want, neither can you."

Crocodiles

689. A crocodile can't stick its tongue out.

690.   Crocodiles can climb trees.

691.   A crocodile can't move its tongue since it is attached to the roof of its mouth.

692.   A crocodile's scales are made of the same material as horse hooves.

693.   They can swim 25mph.

694.   A group of crocodiles is called a congregation or a bask.

695.   When a crocodile sit on river banks with its mouth open, it looks like it is ready to attack. In reality, it's just cooling off.

696.   Crocodiles swallow stones to grind food inside their stomachs because their teeth aren't designed for chewing.

697.   99% of baby crocodiles are eaten in the first year of birth, usually by large fish or lizards.

698.   The Saltwater Crocodile is the largest crocodile species, measuring 24ft in length and weighing one ton.

699.   A crocodile's egg is the same size as a goose's egg.

700.   A crocodile skin purse is worth $15,000.

701.   There are 23 species of crocodile.

702. They have night vision.

703. Crocodiles can live for 80 years.

704. Crocodiles have been around for 240 million years.

705. Some tribes in New Guinea worship crocodiles by scarring their bodies to resemble the skin of the reptile.

Crows

706. Crows have been shown to have the same cognitive skills as a seven-year-old human child.

707. There are 45 species of crow including treepies, corbies, rooks, nutcrackers, bushpies, choughs, magpies, ravens, jackdaws, and the pica pica.

708. Crows pull other animals' tails for fun.

709. Corvid crows attack eagles by dropping stones and pinecones on them.

710. Crows live for 7-14 years.

711. Crows sometimes hitch rides on eagles.

712. Crows will crush ants and rub the entrails over itself like perfume. This technique is known as anting.

713. The Tower of London's ravens are enlisted as soldiers of the United Kingdom. Like human soldiers, the ravens can be dismissed for unsatisfactory conduct. Raven George (who enlisted from 1977-1986) lost his appointment to the Crown, and was retired to Wales after attacking and destroying TV aerials.

714. Pet crows name their owners. They will make a sound for their owner that they will not use for anyone else.

715. Female crows mate for life. Male crows cheat on their partners.

716. Healthy crows will try to help crows that are hurt.

717.	A group of crows is called a murder. This is justified since crows will kill other crows for seemingly no reason.

718.	If a crow dies suspiciously, other crows will investigate it so they can avoid it in the future.

719.	Crows sunbathe because they lack vitamin D.

720.	A group of ravens is called an unkindness.

721.	A group of rooks is called a building.

722.	Crows are the smartest birds in the world.

723.	Jackdaws might be the only birds that stare rivals down. This is extremely odd since the birds' eyes are on the sides of its head, which doesn't make its eyes ideal for staring at an enemy.

Crustaceans

724.   There are 67,000 known crustacean species but experts said there could be as many as 100,000 species.

725.   A crustacean is segmented marine animal with a skeleton on the outside of its body. They have between 6-10 legs and antennas on their head that help them navigate through their environment.

726.   Krill, lobsters, crabs, crayfish, barnacles, and shrimp are the most common types of crustaceans.

727.   A crustacean's exoskeleton is called a carapace.

728.   5,000 crustacean species live in the sea.

729.   Crayfish are the most common freshwater crustacean and are abundant in lakes and ponds.

730.   The woodlouse is a crustacean despite the fact it lives on land.

731.   The most common group of crustaceans are decapods. "Decapod" means "10 legs." Lobsters, prawns, crabs, and crayfish are decapods.

732.   Former president, Teddy Roosevelt, kept lobsters in his dorm room.

733.   The Chengijiangocaris kunmingensis was a crustacean-like creature that lived 520 million years ago. Scientists are fascinated by this animal because its fossilized remains have the oldest and most well-preserved nervous system in history. This is invaluable to biologists because it helps us understand the evolution of the modern nervous system.

Deer

734.   Deer are part of the Cervidae family.

735.   There are 18 types of deer including the moose, reindeer, elk, and other species.

736.   A newborn Chinese Water Deer is small enough to hold in one hand.

737.   The Chinese Water Deer has fangs.

738.   A reindeer's eyes are gold during the summer and blue in winter.

739.   A male deer is a buck. A large male is a stag. A female deer is called a doe or a hind.

740.   The antlers of a Red Deer grow one inch per day.

741.   A moose' antlers are so sensitive, they can feel a fly land on them.

742.   The bigger a moose's antlers are, the better its hearing is.

743.   Most deer are born with white spots but lose them within a year.

744.   A group of deer is called a bunch or a rangale.

745.   The white-tailed deer kill more people in the US than any other animal. These deaths are caused when drivers crash into the deer on the road.

746.   Deer can walk 30 minutes after being born.

747. The word, "deer" is derived from the Medieval English word "der," which means "beast."

748. The smallest deer is the Southern Pudu. It weighs 20lbs and is slightly over 1ft tall.

749. Deer live up to 11 years.

750. If there are no predators around, deer populations can double annually.

751. When deer establish a territory, they will never leave it willingly.

752. Despite its name, the prong-horned antelope is a deer. It has 10x vision, which allows it to see the rings of Saturn on a clear night.

753. In Alaska, it is illegal to whisper in someone's ear while they are hunting for moose.

754. A fully grown deer reaches a height of 7ft.

755. The heaviest deer is the moose, weighing 1,800lbs.

756. All deer have antlers except the Chinese Water Deer.

757. The caribou is the only female deer that has antlers.

758. A deer's antlers grow from boney structures called pedicels.

759. Although many people believe that antlers are shaped like branches, some deer like the muntjacs, have short spikes for antlers.

760. The largest deer ever was the Irish Deer. It went

extinct 11,000 years ago. It was 12ft tall.

761. A moose's vision is so bad, that it sometimes tries to mate with cars.

762. Deer live on every continent except Australia and Antarctica.

763. Deer don't have gall bladders.

764. Deer can't eat hay.

Dinosaurs

765.   Dinosaurs first appeared 230 million years ago.

766.   Dinosaurs died out 65 million years ago. This
means that dinosaurs existed for 165 million years.
Since modern humans have been around for 200,000
years, dinosaurs existed 825 times longer than humans.

767.   The correct term for a long-necked dinosaur is a
sauropod, which means "lizard-footed." Sauropods were
the tallest animals to ever live. Some were over twice as
tall as a giraffe.
         Sauropods are the second most diverse group of
dinosaurs to walk the Earth.

768.   Although the Apatosaurus and the Brachiosaurus
are among the most famous sauropods, there are 150
known types of these dinosaurs.

769.   Although many sources state that dinosaurs
abandoned their eggs like the way lizards do, they
actually cared for their young, much like mammals.

770.   Dinosaurs weren't reptiles. They were a
completely different kind of species. Unlike reptiles,
dinosaurs weren't cold-blooded.
         However, dinosaurs weren't warm-blooded either.
Some animals don't fit into either category such as tuna,
the Great White shark, and certain turtles.

771.   Many dinosaurs could switch from being bipedal
(two-footed) to quadrupedal (four-footed.)

772.   Dinosaurs swallowed large rocks, which would
help them grind their food.

773. Most mammals were very small until dinosaurs went extinct.

774. Dinosaur feathers have been found in amber.

775. Most of the dinosaurs that appeared in the film, Jurassic Park, lived during the Cretaceous period.

776. A baby dinosaur is called a juvenile.

777. A male dinosaur is called a bull. A female dinosaur is called a cow.

778. A Brachiosaurus' tail was so long, it would create a sonic boom when the dinosaur whipped it.

779. Dinosaur remains have recently been discovered on Antarctica.

780. The most dominant sauropod was the Titanosaurus.

781. Most dinosaurs are known from a single bone or tooth.

782. Some biologists would say that dinosaurs are technically not extinct since birds evolved from them.

783. There have been 2,468 dinosaur species discovered.

784. 41% of Americans think dinosaurs and humans lived at the same time.
They didn't.

785. The spikes on a Stegosaurus' tail are called thagomizers. The term was coined by cartoonist, Gary

Larson, in a 1982 Far Side drawing.

786.   The longest complete dinosaur is the 89ft long Diplodocus.

787.   Nobody knows how long dinosaurs lived for.

788.   Most dinosaurs only ate plants.

789.   Meat-eating dinosaurs are called theropods, which means "beast-footed."

790.   Some dinosaurs had skulls that were longer than a car.

791.   In the Jurassic Park film, a Brachiosaurus stands on its hind legs at one point. The Brachiosaurus (and sauropods in general) weren't capable of standing like this.

792.   Some dinosaurs like the Allosaurus didn't reach adulthood until it was 30.

793.   Scorpions, sharks, jellyfish, fish, birds, insects, snakes, turtles, lizards, and crocodiles survived the mass extinction of the dinosaurs.

794.   The first Stegosaurus was found in Colorado. As a result, Colorado is nicknamed the Stegosaurus State.

795.   "Stegosaurus" means "roofed lizard."

796.   Some dinosaurs had nests.

797.   The Stegosaurus had the smallest brain proportion to its size. Although the dinosaur was as large as a van, its brain was the size of a walnut.

798.   The first dinosaur ever discovered was in 1500B.C. in China. The inhabitants found dinosaur teeth and assumed they belonged to a dragon.

799.   The Pentaceratops had the largest skull of all dinosaurs, measuring three meters long.

800.   The Hadrosaurs was the toothiest dinosaur. It had over a thousand teeth.

801.   The Therizinosaurus (which means "reaping lizard") had the longest claws in the dinosaur kingdom, measuring one-meter long.

802.   A newborn human baby's brain is larger than the brain of most adult dinosaurs.

803.   The smartest dinosaur was the Troodon (which means "tooth that wounds.")

804.   Nobody truly knows what dinosaurs looked like and paleontologists have made many silly mistakes over the years.
        Gideon Mantell thought the iguanodon's thumb was its nose. It took 40 years to correct this mistake.

805.   The Ornithomimus was the fastest dinosaur, with a maximum speed of 43mph.

806.   Argentina and China are considered to be the hot spots to find dinosaur remains.

807.   No dinosaurs could fly. All flying creatures like pterosaurs (often incorrectly called pterodactyls) were a separate species.

808. No dinosaurs lived in the sea. Long-necked creatures like the plesiosaurs were reptiles, not dinosaurs.

809. Researchers believe that dinosaurs shed their skin.

810. For years, many scientists believed that dinosaurs had two brains; one in their head and one in their stomach.

811. Most dinosaur fossils have been found near water.

812. The largest carnivorous dinosaur was the Spinosaurus. It is the main antagonist in the film, Jurassic Park III.

813. Scientists don't know if the T-Rex could run or not. If it could, it would be slightly slower than a human.

814. Despite what is depicted in the Jurassic Park films, the Stegosaurus' tail didn't drag across the ground. It was held upright, similar to a cat's tail.

815. The most famous long-necked dinosaur is the Brontosaurus. Two years after it was discovered, it was unveiled as a fake.
    However, when a new sauropod was discovered in 2014, scientists named it the Brontosaurus because everyone already assumes such an animal exists.

816. The majority of dinosaurs were the size of a human or smaller. People believe all dinosaurs were huge simply because larger bones or larger creatures are easier to find.

817. The smallest dinosaur ever was the Baby Mussaurus, which means "mouse lizard." It was four inches tall and

weighed less than a Chihuahua.

818. Most dinosaur eggs were white. Some of them were blueish-green.

819. Google has a T-Rex replica outside their headquarters. His name is Stan.

820. Ray Standford is the greatest dinosaur foorprint-tracker in the world. He has found 300 sets of dinosaur footprints throughout his career.

821. The asteroid that killed the dinosaurs is called Chicxulub.

822. If Chicxulub didn't wipe out the dinosaurs, they still would've gone extinct. Archeologists have stated that dinosaurs were dramatically declining in numbers 65 million years ago and the asteroid simply sped up the process.

Dodos

823.   The dodo was a flightless bird from the island of Mauritius.

824.   Dodos went extinct in 1673.

825.   It weighed 50lbs and stood 3.3ft tall.

826.   Settlers landed on Mauritius in 1598. It only took 75 years for the bird to be wiped out.

827.   Since this bird had no predators, the dodo was completely fearless, which made it easy for settlers to catch them since they didn't run away. In fact, the birds would walk up to settlers while they were eating cooked dodos.

828.   They ate nuts, bulbs, roots, shellfish, crabs, and fallen fruit.

829.   Contrary to popular belief, dodos weren't stupid. CT scans of their skulls show that they were as smart as a pigeon. Pigeons can memorize human faces and have some mathematical abilities.

830.   Dodos weren't just killed by humans. Settlers introduced many animals to the island like dogs, pigs, and cats, which ate the dodos and their eggs.

831.   Modern biologists didn't really know what a dodo looked like until recently. It was only in 2007 that a complete skeleton of a dodo was found.

832.   Many people believe that settlers devoured the dodo because it tasted delicious. This isn't true. The dodo was regularly eaten because it was the easiest

animal to catch.

833.   Dodos seem plump in paintings because they were confined in a cage. Wild dodos were quite thin.

Dogs

834. Dogs aren't mentally capable of feeling guilt. If you screamed at a dog for doing something wrong, it will feel sad, scared, or angry, but never guilty.

835. The chow is the only dog that doesn't have a pink tongue.

836. Dogs live for 10-13 years.

837. The world's oldest dog lived to 29.

838. The most common names for dogs in English-speaking countries are Max and Molly.

839. At the beginning of Paul McCartney's song, A Day in the Life, there's an ultrasonic whistle which can only be heard by dogs.

840. A dog's sense of smell is 10,000 times better than a human's.

841. Abraham Lincoln had a pet dog called Fido. He was assassinated.

842. Three dogs survived the Titanic.

843. A dog and a coyote can mate to give birth to a coydog.

844. Dogs can understand up to 150 words.

845. It is illegal to spay dogs in Norway.

846. The idea that one dog year is the equivalent to seven human years isn't accurate. Different breeds of dog age

at different rates. This applies to most animals.

847. US troops in Vietnam employed 5,000 dogs.

848. Dogs can see images on a HD television. Most dogs couldn't see anything on any previous type of television.

849. 5% of dogs suffer tooth decay. By comparison, 90% of human children suffer tooth decay.

850. Newborn dogs are born blind and deaf. Although they can hear after a few days, they can't see for two weeks.

851. The smallest dog is a female Chihuahua called Brandy. She is six inches long.

852.   A dog's DNA is 99.95% the same as a gray wolf.

853. Dogs usually beg for human food. You would assume a dog does this because it's hungry. In reality, dogs do this to show that they will eat the same food as you to connect and bond with you. Scientists set out two plates of human food, and had a person eat from one of them. After the dog saw the human eat from the plate, it would eat from the same one, even if the other plate had a far larger portion of food.

854. Dogs are pack animals like wolves. If a large group of dogs remained together for an extended period of time without human interaction, they would become feral and violent.

855. Dogs get jealous if their owner shows affection to other dogs.

856. Dogs don't lick you as a sign of love but as a sign of

submission since it perceives you as the alpha.

857. If a dog pulls on a leash, that's not a sign of happiness or eagerness; it's a sign of confusion. Most people speed up their walk when a dog does this but that's not an effective way to train it. The dog needs to understand how the leash works so the dog owner should maintain his or her pace. Also, a dog-owner should never yank the leash as the dog can easily damage a dog's trachea.

858. People assume a dog wags its tail when it is happy. This is true but only when the tail is low, curved, and wagging slowly. It the tail is high and arched, it's aggressive. If the tail wags to the left, it's anxious. If the tail wags to the right, it's curious.

859. When a dog bears its teeth, most owners think it looks like a smile. However, dogs bear their teeth to warn their prey that they will be bitten if they come any closer.

860. A dog sometimes yawns if it sees its owner yawn even if it is not tired.

861. Dogs can get laryngitis if they bark too often.

862. The Great Dane, Zeus, is the largest dog in the world. He's 1.4ft tall when he's sitting and he's 7.4ft when he stands on his hind legs.

863. Corgis are excellent herding dogs.

864. "Dachshund" means "badger dog" in German.

865. Dogs usually yawn because they're stressed.

866. Although dogs can't see as many colors as humans,

they have sharper eyesight.

867. Dogs are mentioned 14 times in the Bible.

868. Don't gaze into a dog's eyes because it will feel threatened. If it gives you the side eye with its whites visible, it might be preparing to bite you.

869. Dogs don't like being hugged because they feel trapped.

870. Cats and horses run away from danger. When a dog feels threatened, it runs to its owner.

871. In 1941, a man from Helsinki was detained after his dog allegedly did the Nazi salute.

872. The Nazis tried to teach dogs how to read.

873. Adolf Hitler created laws against animal cruelty. Near the end of his life, he killed his own dog, Checkers.

874. Chocolate can kill dogs.

875. A dog's shoulder blades are unattached to the rest of the skeleton. This gives it greater flexibility for running.

876. If a puppy is born via caesarean, the mother might reject it.

877. Professional dog tasters (who are human) have to taste all dog brands before allowing them to be sold in pet stores.

878. The phrase "raining cats and dogs" originated in 17th century England. During heavy rainstorms, some

animals would drown and float down the streets, giving the impression that it was literally raining cats and dogs.

879.   There are 400 million dogs in the world.

880.   Kublai Khan owned 5,000 dogs, which is more than anyone in history.

881.   It is illegal to own a dog in Iran.

882.   French poodles originated in Germany, not France.

883.   Alexander the Great founded and named the city of Peritas in memory of his dog.

884.   The Basenji is the only dog that doesn't bark.

885.   William Shakespeare invented the word "watchdog."

886.   Dogs can instinctively make their paws warmer, allowing them to walk through freezing areas.

887.   If a dog goes missing in the US, there's a 93% he or she will return safely.

888.   Zorba is the largest dog ever. He weighed 343lbs and was 8.3ft long.

889.   An average dog can run 19mph, which is slightly slower than a human.

890.   Greyhounds are the fastest dogs in the world. They can run 45mph.

891.　A pair of dogs and their puppies could produce 4,372 puppies in seven years.

892.　The most popular dog in the US is the Labrador Retriever.

893.　Dogs aren't very good at seeing things unless they are moving. If you stood perfectly still in front of a dog from 300 yards away, it wouldn't be able to see you. However, it can easily spot you from a mile away if you wave your arms.

894.　A dog can tell if a human has lung cancer by smelling their breath.

895.　A dog can smell a dead body underwater.

896.　The poodle is the smartest dog.

897.　The Afghan hound is the least intelligent dog.

898.　30% of Dalmatians are deaf in one or both ears.

899.　Dogs are excellent at smelling gas, even if it's 40ft below ground.

900.　US has more dogs than any other country. France has the second-highest number of dogs.

901.　Greyhounds are actually blue. The name "grey hound" comes from the German word "Greishund," which means "old hound."

902.　Dogs learn commands better if a person uses hand gestures while they speak.

903.   Dogs evolved from a weasel-like animal called the Miacis 40 million years ago.

904.   When a dog died in Ancient Egypt, owners would express their sorry by rubbing mud in their hair.

905.   The word "cat" used to mean "dog." It comes from the Latin word "catulus," which means "puppy."

906.   When you rub a dog's ears, you release an endorphin that relaxes their impulses and gives off a sensation that is very similar to marijuana.

907.   The bloodhound is the only animal whose evidence is admissible in court.

Dolphins

908.   Dolphins like to admire themselves in the mirror.

909.   There are 32 species of marine dolphins, four types of river dolphins, and six types of porpoises.

910.   Porpoises have spade-shaped teeth and blunt rounded faces. Dolphins have teeth shaped like rounded cones set in their jaws which extend in a snout or beak.

911.   Dr. Denise Herzing created a dolphin translator called the Cetacean Hearing and Telemetry device. The first thing she decoded was the whistle that dolphins use when they refer to seaweed.

912.   A group of dolphins is called a pod.

913.   Dolphins have lifelong friends who they hang out with. They usually join their friends when they approach a pod of female dolphins. This means dolphins use their friends as wingmen... or finmen.

914.   Dolphins are one of the only animals to mate for pleasure.

915.   Dolphins are one of the only animal that kills its own kind for fun.

916.   Dolphins are one of the only animals to display racist behavior. It is not uncommon for a pod of dolphins to gang up on a porpoise and kill it for no reason except because it looks different.

917.   "Porpoise" comes from the French word "porpais," which means "pork fish."

918.   "Dolphin" comes from the Greek word "delphis," which means "womb."

919.   The US Navy has trained 75 dolphins to detect enemies.

920.   The Marine Mammal Studies Institute trained dolphins to locate trash in water in exchange of fish. One dolphin was smart enough to hide pieces of paper under a rock, tearing off smaller pieces from the paper in order to get more fish out of it.

921.   Although dolphins usually live for 15 years, some can live up to 50 years.

922.   Dolphins sleep with one eye open.

923.   Male dolphins are called bulls and female dolphins are called cows.

924.   Half of a dolphin's brain sleeps at a time.

925.   A two-headed dolphin was discovered on a Turkish beach in 2014.

926.   If you ever see beached dolphin, don't help it back into the water. Dolphins beach themselves when they are sick or injured and are trying to avoid drowning.

927.   Dolphins shed the top layer of their skin every two hours.

928.   Dolphins never drink. All of the water that goes into their mouth is spewed out of their spout. They absorb all of the water they need from the fish they eat.

929. Some dolphins have hair.

930. Dolphins' ancestors used to live on land. Any animal that lived in the sea, then went on land and then went back to the sea is called a re-entrant.

931. Killing a dolphin in Ancient Greece was a capital crime.

932. The killer whale is a dolphin. It is the largest dolphin in the world.

933. Killer whales prey on moose that get too near the coast.

934. Killer whales need to eat the equivalent of three sea lions every day.

935. Killer whales are excellent at team work. If a group of killer whales trap a sea lion on a block of ice, one of the whales will crash into the block, forcing the sea lion to slide into the mouth of another killer whale.

936. Killer whales will launch themselves out of water to catch birds.

937. Killer whales sometimes team up with humpback whales to catch their prey.

938. Killer whales drown whales by shoving them into the ocean.

939. Dolphin teeth are designed for grasping, not chewing.

940. If a dolphin is depressed, it will commit suicide by staying underwater until it drowns. Unlike most

animals, dolphins have to make a conscious effort to breathe.

941.   A dolphin can hold its breath for an hour.

942.   A dolphin's blowhole is technically its nose.

943.   Dolphins can't smell.

944.   Dolphins eat about 33lbs of fish a day.

945.   An average-sized dolphin weighs 260lbs.

946.   Dolphins kill sharks by stabbing them with their snout.

947. Dolphins are the second smartest animals on Earth and are able to understand 50 English words. However, Carl Sagan argued that dolphins are smarter than humans because "no human being has been reported to have learned Dolphinese."

948. Dolphins can communicate over the telephone and can tell which dolphin they are speaking to because they can recognize each other's' pitch.

__Donkeys__

949.   Because of the way a donkey's eyes are placed, it can see all of its legs at the same time.

950.   A group of donkeys is called a coffle, a drove, or a pace.

951.   The donkey was once called "cardophagus," which means "thistle-eater."

952.   There are 41 million donkeys worldwide.

953.   Over 25% of all of the donkeys in the world live in China.

954.   A mule is a cross between a horse and a donkey. It is a common pet in the US.

955.   A male donkey is a called a jack. A female donkey is called a jenny.

956.   Donkeys live for 40 years.

Ducks

957.   Ducks are part of the Anatidae bird family, which also includes swans and geese.

958.   Feeding bread to ducks can be very dangerous to their health.

959.   A male duck is a drake. A female duck is a hen.

960.   A group of ducks is called a raft.

961.   All ducks have waterproof feathers. When a duck dives underwater, its downy underlayer of feathers stay completely dry.

962.   Ducklings can leave the nest within half an hour of hatching from their eggs.

963.   Ducks eat grass, plants, insects, seeds, fruit, fish, and crustaceans.

964.   A duck's bill is designed to forage in mud and to strain food from water.

965.   Very few ducks quack. Most ducks squeak, grunt, groan, chirp, whistle, bray, or growl. Drakes usually don't make any sound.

966.   Ducks were domesticated 500 years ago.

967.   There are 40 types of domestic duck.

968.   Ducks usually live for about six years. The oldest duck ever lived for 20 years.

969. The word "duck" is derived from the Old English word for "diver."

970. Its main predator is the heron.

971. They can sleep with one eye open.

Eagles

972.   Some eagles can see 3.6 times more acutely than a human. If you had the same eyesight as an eagle, you could see an ant on the ground from the roof of a 10-story building.

973.   There are 60 kinds of eagles.

974.   Eagles usually lay two eggs at once. However, when the bigger egg hatches, the baby eagle usually kills its sibling once it hatches. Adult eagles do not intervene.

975.   The Harpy Eagle and the Philippine Eagle are so large, they can carry monkeys and deer in their talons.

976.   A Golden Eagle will kill a turtle by grabbing it with its talons and then dropping it from a large distance in order to crack the turtle's shell open.

977.   A group of eagles is called a convocation.

978.   A baby eagle is called a fledging.

979.   In the 1700s, there were about 400,000 bald eagles in the US. Now, there are only 70,000.

Elephants

980.   Elephants are scared of bees.

981.   Elephants can hear each other's' trumpeting calls for up to five miles.

982.   Despite what cartoons depict, elephants don't like peanuts.

983.   The largest elephant is the African Elephant. The largest one ever was 13ft high and weighed 24,000lbs. It is also the largest land animal.

984.   Elephants pour sand on their bodies to stop themselves getting sunburnt.

985.   A single elephant tooth can weight 9lbs.

986.   Poachers kill elephants for the ivory in their tusks. However, elephants can be born without tusks, which means that poachers will leave them alone. What's interesting is that if two tuskless elephants mate, the chances of them giving birth to a tuskless elephant is very high. Because of this, tuskless elephants have been increasing over the years.

987.   African Elephants have the best sense of smell in the animal kingdom.

988.   An elephant's trunk has no bones and is made up of 40,000 muscles.

989.   Elephants only sleep two or three hours a day.

990.   An adult African Elephant can eat up to 660lbs of food a day and can drink 160 liters of water a day.

991.   An elephant's tusks can weigh up to 441lbs.

992.   Elephants are pregnant for two years.

993.   Elephants have calves every 4-9 years.

994.   One relative of the elephant that went extinct millions of years ago was the Platybelodon. It looked similar to a modern elephant except its mouth resembled a gargantuan shovel. It had flat teeth that helped the creature scoop food into its mouth.

995.   One of the most expensive coffee brands is made from the dung of Thai elephants.

996.   The brain of an African Elephant weighs 11lbs, which is more than any other land animal.

997.   Elephants can suffer from post-traumatic stress syndrome.

998.   Elephants rarely get cancer because they have 40 genes to suppress tumors. By comparison, humans only have two of these genes.

999.   An adult Asian Elephant can hold 8.5 liters of water in its trunk.

1000.   Elephants bury their dead and have funerals.

1001.   Elephants suffer depression after their friends die.

1002.   95 elephants are killed daily in Africa.

1003.   Elephants can detect rain 150 miles away.

1004. When humans first saw an elephant skull, they thought it belonged to a Cyclops. This is because the skull doesn't indicate that the animal has a trunk.

1005. An elephant can die of a broken heart. If their mate dies, they can lay down, refuse to eat, shedding tears until they starve to death.

1006. Elephants are one of the worst animals at adapting to zoo life. Although most animals live longer in zoos than in the wild, African Elephants in captivity tend to live for 17 years. An African elephant in the wild normally lives for 50 years. Researchers are unsure why this happens.

1007. The oldest elephant ever was 82 years old.

1008. Poachers used the code word "banana" when referring to elephants, ivory, or tusks.

Endangered Species

1009.   On July 19th 2012, the IUCN Red List of Threatened Species concluded that there are 19,817 endangered species in the world today. However, this is only based on the 3% of animals that the IUCN researched.

1010.   There are 3,947 critically endangered species. A critically endangered species will go extinct very soon unless drastic measures are taken.

1011.   In September 2016, the Giant Panda was finally removed from the critically endangered animal list. It is now in the vulnerable category.

1012.   Of the 19,817 endangered species, 41% are amphibians, 25% are mammals, and 13% are birds.

1013.   The pangolin (also known as the spiny anteater) is the most trafficked animal in the world. These strange-looking mammals are sold in China and Vietnam because the citizens believe the animals' scales cure fevers (which is untrue.) Sadly, this superstition is driving this poor creature to extinction. Over a million have been killed over the last decade.

1014.   The Clarion Night Snake was first seen in 1936. It wasn't seen for decades and so, scientists assumed it went extinct. In fact, some biologists doubted that the snake ever existed and demanded it should be removed from the record. It was found again in 2013 on Clarion Island.

1015.   The Amur Leopard is the rarest big cat in the world. There are only 70 remaining in the wild.

1016.   The trees that the Sumatran Orangutans live in have reduced in numbers over the last 30 years as humans chop them down to make space for plantations. Biologists believe that if 1% of the remaining female orangutans die out, it could trigger the animal's extinction.

Worst still, this will cause the extinction of several trees as the species play a vital role in the forest's seed dispersal.

1017.   The Northern White Rhino is now considered extinct in the wild and the remaining rhinos only exist in captivity with 24/7 supervision.

1018.   There are less than 20 Hainan gibbons left on Earth.

1019.   There are four Red River turtles left on Earth.

1020.   The black soft-shell turtle, the Hawaiian crow, the scimitar Oryx, and the axolotl no longer exist in the wild. They are only alive today because they are protected in captivity.

Extinct Animals

1021.   An endling is the last animal of a species. Once it dies, that animal will become extinct. One such endling is Toughie the Rabbs' Fringe-Limbed Tree Frog. His partner died in 2009. When he dies, his species will no longer exist.

1022.   Stromatolites were the earliest known lifeforms. These sea-dwelling micro-organisms lived 3.5 billion years ago.

1023.   Animals have been going extinct for millions of years. However, because of human intervention, animals are going extinct 5,000 times faster than the natural extinction rate.

1024.   Humans have caused at least 322 animal extinctions in the last 500 years.

1025.   A Mass Extinction is an event that wipes out a majority of the animals on Earth. There have been five Mass Extinctions throughout history.
i) The Permian Period
ii) The Triassic Period
iii) The Cretaceous Period
iv) The Jurassic Period
v) The Holocene Period is the current era.
        The Permian, Triassic, and Cretaceous animals died out due to environmental changes.
        The Jurassic animals died after an asteroid collided into the Earth.
        The Holocene Period is where species can become extinct because of one animal – us. This era probably started when our ancestors wiped out the mammoth.

1026.   99% of every creature that has ever lived is now extinct.

1027.   Sometimes, an animal is believed to be extinct but it turns out that it has survived. Examples include the Christmas Island Shrew, the Flying Fox, and the Rock Rat.

1028.   Some animals become extinct in one area but are living in other parts of the world. This is known as a local extinction.

1029.   The most common reason animals have gone extinct throughout history is due to the inability to adapt to a changing environment.

1030.   The quagga went extinct in 1883. It looked like a horse with the head of a zebra. Only one photograph of the animal exists today. It was the first extinct animal to have its DNA studied.

1031.   The Tasmanian Tiger (or Tasmanian Wolf) went extinct at some point in the 20th century.

1032.   The Californian Grizzly Bear went extinct in 1924.

1033.   The Baiji River Dolphin went extinct in 2006.

1034.   The Liverpool Pigeon went extinct in 2008.

1035.   The Black Andean Toad went extinct in 2008.

1036.   The Pyrenean Ibex goat is the only animal to go extinct twice! It died out in 2000, was cloned back to life, but perished soon after.

1037.   The Western Black Rhino went extinct in 2011.

1038.   Humans kill 1,776 animals for food every second.

1039.   By the year 2050, 30 to 50% of all species could be near extinction.

1040.   The greatest leap in evolution took place 375 million years ago when the first aquatic creature walked on land, kick-starting life above sea level. This creature is known as the Tikaalik. This amphibian-fish had gills and lungs. It is known as the Grandfather of Tetrapods. A tetrapod is a four-limbed vertebrate.

1041.   One of the most famous extinct animals is the trilobite. Over 20,000 species of trilobite have been discovered by archeologists. They went extinct 250 million years ago.

1042.   There's a genus of trilobite called Han, which contains only one known species – Han Solo.

1043.   Global warming could lead to 16% of animals going extinct.

1044.   The Purussaurs had the strongest bite in the animal kingdom. This crocodile-like creature was longer than a school bus and weighed over eight tons. They ate 88lbs of meat a day. They went extinct about eight million years ago.

1045.   The Dunkleosteu was a fish that lived 380 million years ago. It was 33.4ft long and weighed 3.6 tons. It could open its jaw in 0.02 seconds, which would create a vacuum, sucking in nearby prey. Its bite was twice as strong as a Great White Shark and it preyed on animals larger than itself. Most importantly, it is the first known large predator.

1046. The Arhthropleura was the largest land invertebrate to ever live. This colossal millipede-like creature could reach a height of 7.5ft tall and weigh over 1,000lbs. They went extinct about 280 million years ago.

1047. One of the goofiest-looking animals ever was a crab-like marine creature called the Opabinia. This creature lived around 520 million years ago. It had a spoon-shaped bill, five eyes, a trilobite-like body, and a fan-shaped tail.
     When it was first revealed to the scientific community in 1912, the audience burst out laughing.

1048. Our ancestor, Australopithecus (aka Lucy,) existed 3.6 million years ago and went extinct after 900,000 years. By comparison, humans have only existed for 200,000 years.

Falcons

1049. Although falcons look like they are related to eagles and hawks, the bird that they are most related to is the parrot.

1050. Falconry has existed for over 4,000 years.

1051. There are 39 species of falcon.

1052. There are five kinds of falcon in the US – Gyrfalcon, Peregrine, Merlin, Prairie, and American Kestrel.

1053. They can migrate as far as 10,000 miles.

1054. Their bodies can weigh as little as 2lbs.

1055. They can spot their prey up to a mile away.

1056. They usually don't travel further than 30 miles from their nest. They don't like other falcons within three miles of their nest site.

1057. Their eggs can be pink or red.

1058. The male and female incubate the eggs.

1059. Baby falcons are called eyasses.

1060. A male falcon is called a terzel. A female is simply called a falcon.

1061. Falconry developed because falcons could kill animals beyond the range of a hunter's weapon.

1062. Falcons tend to kill their prey while in flight.

1063.   They usually prey on ducks, pigeons, and gulls.

1064.   The name "falcon" is derived from the Latin word, "Falco Peregrinus," which means "wandering traveler."

1065.   Genghis Khan had 10,000 falconers at his disposal.

1066.   The Peregrine Falcon is the largest falcon. It is also the fastest animal in the world. When it descends on its prey, it moves at 230mph. That's twice as fast as anything other animal and triple the speed of a cheetah. It kills its prey on impact with a balled foot. Some people call this attack a Falcon Punch.

Ferrets

1067.   Ferrets are a part of the Mustelidae family, which includes weasels, minks, otters, polecats, skunks, and badgers.

1068.   The word "ferret" is derived from the Latin word "fur," which means "little thief."

1069.   Ferrets were domesticated thousands of years ago to help hunters' flush rabbits out of their holes.

1070.   Like skunks, ferrets can emit odors when they are scared.

1071.   Ferret owners have their pets de-scented to prevent them from stinking up the house.

1072.   Ferrets are the only members of the weasel family that have been domesticated.

1073.   They can sleep for up to 20 hours a day.

1074.   Baby ferrets are called kits.

1075.   Ferrets are born white. They become their permanent color when they are three months old.

1076.   The Black-Footed Ferret was thought to be extinct until it was recently rediscovered in America.

1077.   When they are happy, they make a clucking noise known as dooking.

1078.   Like a dog, they wag their tail when they are excited.

1079.   Male ferrets are called hobs. Females are called jills. A castrated male is called a gib. A spayed female is a sprite.

1080.   Crossbreeding ferrets is discouraged because it makes them prone to Waardenburg syndrome, which renders the poor creatures deaf.

1081.   If a female ferret doesn't mate and has not been spayed, she can produce so much estrogen, that she can clot to death.

1082.   Engineers have trained ferrets to carry cables through tunnels and pipes that are too small for humans.

1083.   It's illegal to own a ferret in Hawaii, New York, Washington DC, and California.

1084.   Ferrets become geriatric when they are only six years old.

1085.   It is the most common mammalian pet in the US apart from the cat and the dog.

1086.   Although ferrets have been domesticated for over 2,000 years, they have been a popular pet in the US for only 30 years.

1087.   Queen Elizabeth II owns an albino ferret, which appears in one of her portraits.

1088.   Ferret legging is a contest where participants have two live ferrets dropped into their trousers that are then sealed at the waist and ankles so the creatures can't escape. The animals will then claw and bite to try and free themselves. The winner is the person who can keep the ferrets in their trousers the longest.

Also, each participant is not allowed to wear underwear.

Although most people only last a few minutes, the world record is over five hours.

Fish

1089.   There are 32,000 species of fish.

1090.   When Anglerfish mate, the male latches on and fuses with the female, losing his internal organs until both fish share a bloodstream.

1091.   The Channa Andrao is a fish that can slither on land for almost 500 meters. It's nicknamed Fishzilla. They are one of the few fish that breathe air. They can live on land for up to four days.
        When people see them, they usually mistake the fish for a snake.

1092.   A baby fish is called a fry.

1093.   The opah is the only warm-blooded fish in the world.

1094.   Fish have existed for 530 million years.

1095.   Some fish can swim backwards.

1096.   80% of fish mass has been lost in the last century.

1097.   Clown fish are always born male. They change their gender throughout their entire lives.

1098.   Puffer fish are the most poisonous animal on Earth apart from the Arrow Frog. They have enough poison to kill 30 people. Its toxin is 1,200 times deadlier than cyanide.

1099.   10% of all fish species lie within the Great Barrier Reef.

1100.   Thousands of marine creatures die every year by swallowing plastic bags that resemble jellyfish.

1101.   The Gar is a fish that has an alligator-like snout and teeth. It is considered to be one of the scariest looking fish in the world.

1102.   Fish that live in polluted areas lose their sense of smell.

1103.   Many brands of lipstick contain fish scales.

1104.   The Goliath Tigerfish launches itself out of the air to catch birds in mid-flight. It is so vicious, it eats sharks and crocodiles.

1105.   Most fish can taste without opening their mouths.

1106.   Anglerfish use a lure to attract prey. The lure is called an esca.

1107.   An anglerfish's mouth is so big, it can eat prey twice its size.

1108.   Many fish species change their gender throughout their lives. 33% of male fish in British rivers are changing their gender to counter pollution that affects males.

1109.   The Polytechnic Institute of New York University created a fish-shaped robot and put it in water to see how other fish would react to it. The robot became the fish's leader.

1110.   Fish can drown.

1111. Koi fish can live for over 200 years.

1112. A Remora uses its dorsal fin to latch onto larger fish so it doesn't have to waste energy swimming. They are the hitchhikers of the sea.

1113. The Northern Stargazer is a fish that waits in the sand. When its prey come near, the fish shocks it with its eyes.

1114. Catfish can grow 13ft long and weigh 880lbs.

1115. The Sheepheadfish has human-looking teeth.

1116. Lungfish can live out of water for several years. They have gills and one lung.

1117. Although enamel is known as the biological cement that caps teeth, it used to serve as armor on fish 400 million years ago.

1118. Fish moan, grunt, croak, boom, hiss, whistle, creak, shrike, and wail to communicate to each other.

1119. A fish's jaw is not connected to its head.

1120. Most fish can see in color.

1121. Flying fish can glide 50 meters and reach heights up of to six meters.

1122. A group of fish is called a school.

1123. Schools can have over a million fish.

1124. The fish in the center of a school controls what

direction the group moves in.

1125.   Some fish don't have scales.

1126.   Taiwanese Cavefish are the only fish that climb up walls.

1127.   Batfish play dead when predators approach.

1128.   Four-eyed fish can see above and below water at the same time.

1129.   Salmon can find the river they were born in.

1130.   Although piranhas have a bad reputation, they are harmless to humans. In fact, some of them are vegetarian.

1131.   Fish were the first vertebrates with bony skeletons to appear on Earth. However, the first fish didn't have scales or fins.

1132.   A trout will go into a trance if it is tickled.

1133.   According to marine expert, Stephen Jay Gould, fish are technically not a species, but thousands of subspecies.

    Although many fish look alike, they have very little in common genetically. A salmon has more genetic similarities to a camel than a hagfish.

    When we think of a fish, we mean, "any vertebrate that lives underwater that isn't a mammal or reptile."

Flamingoes

1134.   Many sources say flamingos are pink because they eat shrimp. This is untrue. Flamingoes are pink because they eat algae.

1135.   Flamingos eat when their head is upside down.

1136.   They have 19 vertebrae in a flamingo's neck.

1137.   Although there are six species of flamingo, they are divided into many subspecies.

1138.   The word, "flamingo" comes from the Spanish word, "flamenco," which means "fire."

1139.   They can fly at 35mph.

1140.   Flamingo chicks have straight beaks. After a few months, its beak will develop its "break" curve, which will allow them to eat on their own.

1141.   Flamingo chicks are born white or grey.

1142.   Flamingos can be pink, orange, or red.

1143.   They eat shrimp, plankton, algae, and crustaceans.

1144.   The largest flamingo is the Greater Flamingo, standing 5ft tall. Despite its height, it only weighs 8lbs.

1145.   Its legs can be up to 50 inches long.

1146.   A group of flamingoes is called a flock, a flamboyance, or a regiment.

1147.   A flock can contain over a million flamingoes.

1148.   The egg yolks of a flamingo are pink.

1149.   They can live up to 50 years.

Fleas

1150.   Fleas are wingless insects that rely on jumping vast distances to reach its desired location.

1151.   The flea can jump 13 inches horizontally or seven inches vertically.

1152.   The flea is the best jumper in the animal kingdom in proportion to its size apart from the froghopper. If a man had the jumping power of a flea, he could jump 295ft horizontally or 160ft vertically.

1153.   They feed off the blood of humans, birds, and reptiles.

1154.   There are 2,000 species of fleas.

1155.   The flea that lives on humans is called the Pulex irritans.

1156.   Fleas can survive 100 days without eating.

1157.   Fleas can cause anemia in pets.

1158.   The most common flea in the Western world is the Cat flea. This pest can be found in cats and dogs.

1159.   A female flea consumes 15 times its own body weight daily.

1160.   Fleas have existed for 100 million years.

1161.   The female flea can lay 2,000 eggs in its lifetime.

1162.   22-million-year-old fleas have been discovered in the Dominican Republic in 2015 that harbored the Y.

pestis parasite, which caused the Bubonic Plague in Europe during the Middle Ages.

Flies

1163.   Biologists have stated that flies have evasive capabilities that rival military aircraft.

1164.   House flies hum in the F key.

1165.   A fly's brain creates an escape plan 100 milliseconds after it sees a threat. Their wings have aerodynamic force, which allows them to change course with a single wing beat. This is why it is nearly impossible to hit a fly.

1166.   The smaller most animals are, the slower they sense time. This is why flies are almost impossible to hit.

1167.   There are 120,000 species of flies in the world.

1168.   One housefly can lay 600 eggs in their lifetime.

1169.   Flies live for 21 days.

1170.   If a fly is infected with a parasite, it will try and kill it by drinking alcohol.

1171.   Its mouth is designed for lapping and sucking, not biting or chewing.

1172.   They can beat their wings 200 times per second.

1173.   Their eyes have 4,000 lenses.

1174.   They rely on their sense of smell.

1175.   Flies defecate every few minutes.

1176.   Flies caused $10 billion worth of agricultural products every year according to the US Department of Agriculture.

1177.   A baby fly is called a maggot. Although they look disgusting, they are very effective against flesh wounds, especially for burn victims, since maggots only eat dead flesh.

Foxes

1178.   A male fox is called a tod. A female fox is a vixen.

1179.   A group of foxes is called a skulk or a leash.

1180.   The Middle East had pet foxes before they had pet dogs.

1181.   Although it's a part of the dog family, foxes are very similar to cats. Like a cat, foxes can retract their claws. No other animal in the dog family can do this. Like a cat, foxes have spines on their tongues.

1182.   The most common fox is the Red Fox.

1183.   The animal in the Firefox logo isn't a fox. It's a Red Panda.

1184.   The fox harnesses the planet's magnetic field to hunt. Although it's invisible to us, a fox can actually see the magnetic field as a ring of shadow.

1185.   They can make 40 different sounds.

1186.   Although there are at least 37 species that are called "foxes," only 12 types actually belong to the Vulpes genus of "true foxes."

1187.   Charles Darwin discovered a fox. It is now known as the Darwin's Fox.

1188.   A vixen gives birth to an average of six pups. Up to 11 pups can be born in one litter.

1189.   The Fennec Fox is the smallest fox in the world. It weighs 3lbs and is the size of a kitten.

1190.   They eat berries, worms, spiders, mice, and birds. City foxes eat rubbish that people leave out.

1191.   Grey Foxes are the only animals in the dog family that can climb trees.

1192.   Foxes weigh about 13lbs.

1193.   The Arctic Fox might have the highest resistance to cold of any mammal. It doesn't even shiver until it's -70 degrees Celsius.

1194.   There's a fox-wolf hybrid in Asia called a dhole. It's the only animal of the Vulpes family (wolves, jackals, foxes, etc.) that communicates by whistling.

<u>Frogs</u>

1195.   The Glass Frog looks astonishingly like Kermit the Frog from The Muppets.

1196.   Although Kermit the Frog is the most famous fictional frog character, he was originally a turquoise lizard puppet.

1197.   The Limnonectes larvapartus is the only frog that gives birth to live tadpoles. Its name means "marsh swimmer that gives birth to larvae."

1198.   Many people believe frogs have a long snapping tongue like a chameleon thanks to many cartoon depictions. In reality, frogs have a short, backward tongue.

1199.   When a frog swallows, its eyeballs move to the inside of its mouth to help push the food down its throat.

1200.   The Arrow Frog is the most poisonous animal on Earth. It has enough poison to kill a thousand people. They are so-called because hunters use to dip their arrows into the frog before firing them at their enemy, guaranteeing a kill.

   The animal is so poisonous, that a human will die just by being near it.

1201.   There are only two venomous frogs – the Arrow Frog and the Brunos' Casque-Head Frog. Venomous frogs never intentionally kill animals with their poison.

1202.   After the Disney film, The Princess and the Frog, was released, there were dozens of reports of children being hospitalized with salmonella after kissing frogs.

1203.　　The Khorat Frog is the most vicious frog in the world. It has fangs, which are strong enough to hurt humans. This frog eats small birds.

1204.　　The Horror Frog deserves its name. When threatened, it will break its own toes to force its inner-claws to pierce through them.

1205.　　The Alaskan Wood Frog freezes in winter and its heart completely stops. In spring, it unthaws and returns to normal.

1206.　　Immediately after a tadpole transforms, it is known as a froglet.

1207.　　The Pristimantis mutabilis is a frog that can change its appearance more efficiently than a chameleon. Not only can it change its color to match its surroundings, but also its texture. It can make its skin smooth or bumpy or spiky.

1208.　　In 2010, the Microhyla nepenthicola was discovered. It is the smallest frog in the world and one of the tiniest vertebrates ever discovered. It was actually discovered 100 years ago but scientists assumed it was a baby version of another frog. It measures 3mm.

1209.　　There are 4,800 types of frogs. Only one species of frog can ribbit.

1210.　　Frogs swallow their food whole.

1211.　　They can't live in saltwater.

1212.   Contrary to myth, frogs or toads can't give you warts.

1213.   The gastric brooding frog is the only animal that gives birth through its mouth.

Geese

1214.   Geese have fangs.

1215.   Geese are a part of the Anseriformers family, which includes all waterfowl. Geese are the largest waterfowl apart from swans.

1216.   A group of geese is called a gaggle or a plump. When geese are airborne, the group is known as a skein of geese.

1217.   A male goose is called a gander. A female is simply called a goose.

1218.   Despite their docile appearance, geese are vicious. If a human comes near their territory, the goose will hiss and bite the intruder.

1219.   They will fly up to 3,000 miles to reach their birth place every year.

1220.   They are very protective of their gaggle and will protect one another if one of the group falls ill.

1221.   They will travel over 100 miles for water.

1222.   The most common goose is the Canadian Goose.

1223.   Geese live for about 25 years.

1224.   A goose's main predators are foxes, owls, raccoons, and turtles.

1225.   There are 30 species of goose.

1226.   A goose's egg hatches the same day it's laid.

1227. Adult geese molt in June. They can't fly until they stop molting.

1228. Geese can fly when they are only two months old.

1229. Geese can lay 50 eggs per year.

1230. A baby goose is called a gosling.

1231. Parent geese will walk with their goslings in a straight line, with a parent in front and a parent at the back.

Giraffes

1232.　Giraffes only need to sleep for 30 minutes a day. Some of them can sleep for as little as five minutes a day.

1233.　Giraffes don't have a long neck to help them eat from tall trees. Most giraffes eat plants from the ground. Even when there is food at the top of trees, giraffes are far more inclined to eat from lower shrubs.

Their long neck is used for fighting. A giraffe uses its neck like a swinging club against rival giraffes. The longer the neck, the bigger the swing, and the more damage it can do to its rivals. Giraffes with smaller necks have been weeded out by natural selection as the long-necked giraffes were the superior fighters.

1234.　Although giraffes have vocal chords, they rarely make sounds.

1235.　Giraffes are the tallest animals in the world. Males can grow 18ft tall.

1236.　Giraffes rarely drink because they receive most of the water they need from the plants that they eat.

1237.　A giraffe's leg is about 6ft high.

1238.　A giraffe's foot is 1ft across. That's about the same size as a dinner plate.

1239.　The giraffe is one of the few vertebrate species that can't yawn.

1240.　50% of giraffe calves don't live longer than six months.

1241.   Giraffes have gone extinct in seven African countries.

1242.   In Mozambique, power lines have to be at least 39ft high so giraffes don't collide into them.

1243.   A giraffe's intestine measure over 230ft.

1244.   A male giraffe can weigh 4,250lbs.

1245.   Nobody can agree on how many species of giraffe there are. Most geneticists believe there are 9-11 species.

1246.   A giraffe's neck can measure up to 6ft.

1247.   Its tongue is black and measures 1.5ft long.

1248.   A giraffe can lick the inside of its ears with its tongue.

1249.   At least seven species of giraffe are now extinct in Africa.

Goats

1250.   A goat and a sheep can have a baby called a geep.

1251.   Goats have rectangular pupils.

1252.   The goat was the first animal that humans used for milk consumption.

1253.   The Alpine Ibex goat (also known as a Steinbock or Bouquetin) has such good balance, that it can walk up an almost vertical mountain. They can effortlessly jump 6ft upward while on steep mountains.

1254.   Goat milk is the world's most consumed milk by humans.

1255.   There are 210 breeds of goat.

1256.   A group of goats is called a trip.

1257.   A male goat is called a billy or a buckling. A female goat is called a nanny or a doeling.

1258.   China has more goats than any other country in the world – 170 million.

1259.   There is a story of a 9th century Ethiopian goat herder called Kaldi who noticed that his goats would become excited when they ate a specific bean. When he consumed the beans himself, he felt a sudden burst of energy. Soon after, he began mass-producing the beans and made a fortune. The beans became the coffee plant. Although this story isn't irrefutable, it's possible that all of humanity's coffee is owed to a bunch of goats.

Goldfish

1260.   Goldfish don't have stomachs.

1261.   They don't urinate. Instead, they filter out ammonia using their gills.

1262.   Goldfish can lay thousands of eggs at once. Only a small portion of the eggs will be fertilized.

1263.   Goldfish eat plants, insects, crustaceans, and fish.

1264.   During the 17th century in the UK, goldfish were a common anniversary present.

1265.   If you see a goldfish floating at the top of a fish tank, it's constipated, not dead. Within three or four days, it'll be back to normal.

1266.   Touching a goldfish will damage the slime coat that protects its skin, which might make the fish develop an infection.

1267.   Although many people think goldfish have a three-second memory, they can remember things for up to a month.

1268.   Goldfish can see infrared radiation, which is invisible to the human eye.

1269.   There are 12 types of goldfish.

1270.   The most common name for a goldfish is Jaws.

1271.   A group of goldfish is called a troubling.

Gorillas

1272.   Gorillas make new nests every night. The gorilla makes the largest nest in the animal kingdom.

1273.   There are two kinds of gorilla- the Eastern Gorilla and the Western Gorilla. Each of these are divided into two subspecies – Eastern Lowland Gorilla, Eastern Mountain Gorilla, Western Lowland Gorilla, and the Cross River Gorilla.

1274.   The Western Lowland gorilla is the most common gorilla. There is up to 200,000 of these gorillas in the world.

1275.   A gorilla will hum if it enjoys its meal.

1276.   They live for about 37 years.

1277.   Gorillas are the only apes that aren't great climbers.

1278.   Gorillas can catch colds and other illnesses from humans and vice versa.

1279.   A baby gorilla is called an infant.

1280.   The word "gorilla" is derived from a Greek word, which means "a tribe of hairy women."

1281.   Gorillas burp when they are happy.

1282.   The scientific name for a Western Lowland gorilla is Gorilla gorilla gorilla.

1283.   They can make 25 different sounds.

1284.   They eat 70lbs worth of food a day.

1285.   They eat bamboo, fruit, leafy plants, and small insects.

1286.   Gorillas are able to learn sign language. Koko the gorilla was able to use 1,000 signs and she could understand 2,000 words.

1287.   Gorillas usually have one baby every five years.

1288.   A female gorilla will only have three or four babies throughout her lifetime.

1289.   Female gorillas use a type of "baby talk" to communicate with their infants.

1290.   Andrew Battle was the first person in the Western Hemisphere to see a gorilla. When he tried to describe it to other explorers, they didn't believe him.

Grasshoppers

1291.   A grasshopper can leap 20 times the length of its own body.

1292.   If you had the same jumping strength as a grasshopper, you could leap the length of a football field.

1293.   When people hear the word "grasshopper," they think of colorful, music-playing insects.

When people hear the word "locust," they probably think of a swarm of insects that devours plants and destroys entire farms.

What many people don't know is that the locust and the grasshopper are the same thing. Although there's different types of grasshoppers, the locust's official name is the short-horned grasshopper.

1294.   Their ears are on their bellies.

1295.   Although they can hear, they can't distinguish pitches very well.

1296.   Grasshoppers have existed for 300 million years. They were around long before the dinosaurs existed.

1297.   They have five eyes.

1298.   Grasshoppers spit at their enemies.

1299.   They play music by rubbing their legs. This is known as stridulating.

1300.   Although they rely on jumping, they can fly.

1301.   Grasshoppers cause $1.5 billion worth of damage

in food crops every year.

1302.   Grasshoppers are eaten in many countries because their bodies are filled with protein.

Guinea Pigs

1303.   They originated in the Andes.

1304.   Guinea pigs were domesticated in 5000B.C.

1305.   The reason why they are called guinea pigs is because they were originally sold for a guinea (an old English coin.)

1306.   Males are called boars and females are sows.

1307.   Guinea pigs have been used as medicine in South America. Even today, guinea pigs will be rubbed on people who suffer from arthritis and jaundice.

1308.   Baby guinea pigs are called pups.

1309.   Guinea pigs can make ultrasonic sounds, which can't be heard by humans.

1310.   If a female is being bothered by a male, she sometimes squirts urine at him.

1311.   If a female doesn't give birth within six months, she will become infertile.

1312.   Like humans, guinea pigs can't produce vitamin C, which is a pretty rare trait in mammals.

1313.   Queen Elizabeth I owned a guinea pig, which led to them becoming popular pets in the UK.

1314.   Their teeth never stop growing so they need to grind them down.

1315.   A woman in Kent, England had two pet guinea

pigs. She didn't have them neutered because she had no idea how quickly they reproduce. Within four years, she had 100 guinea pigs.

1316.   Autistic children from the ages of 5-12 show a massive decrease in stress when interacting with guinea pigs.

1317.   Millions of years ago, the guinea pigs' ancestor, the Josephoartigasia monesi, stood 5ft high, weighed a ton, and was 10ft long. It had the same bite force as a tiger.

1318.   They are allergic to penicillin.

1319.   Although some pet stores sell leashes for guinea pigs, they should never be used as guinea pigs have delicate spines.

1320.   Guinea pigs march in single file, with the largest in front and the youngest in the middle.

1321.   The scientific name for a guinea pig is Cavia porcellus, which means "little pig."

1322.   Truffles was a guinea pig that held the Guinness World Record for the longest leap for his species when he cleared a gap of 18.89 inches in April 2012.

Hamsters

1323.   Most animals are diurnal (active during the day) or nocturnal (active during the night.) However, hamsters are crepuscular, which means they are active during the twilight hours.

1324.   The largest hamster is the European Hamster, which grows over 1ft long.

1325.   The Roborovsku Dwarf Hamster is the smallest hamster, measuring two inches long.

1326.   Hamsters can store food in their cheeks to eat later.

1327.   They usually live for four years.

1328.   Hamsters run up to eight miles at night on a wheel.

1329.   Although most females have seven pups at once, they can have as many as 24 in a single litter.

1330.   There are five hamster species that are kept as pets – Roborovski, Syrian, Campbell's Dwarf, Chinese, and Winter White Russian Dwarf Hamsters.

Hawks

1331.   A baby hawk is called a eyas.

1332.   A group of hawks is called an aerie. When they migrate in large groups, it is known as a cauldron of hawks.

1333.   There are 270 species of hawk.

1334.   The largest hawk is the Ferruginous hawk. It only weighs 5lbs.

1335.   Their eyesight is eight times better than a human.

1336.   The female is larger than the male, which is rare in the animal kingdom.

1337.   Most hawks pair for life.

1338.   The Harris Hawk is the only bird of prey that hunts in packs.

1339.   They eat frogs, insects, squirrels, rats, snakes, rabbits, and birds.

1340.   Male falcons dance in the air for 10 minutes in order to impress potential mates.

Hedgehogs

1341.   A baby hedgehog is called a hoglet.

1342.   A group of hedgehogs is called an array.

1343.   Hedgehogs are illegal in seven US states.

1344.   Each hedgehog can have as many as 7,000 quills.

1345.   There are 17 species of hedgehog.

1346.   Unlike porcupines, hedgehog spikes aren't barbed or poisonous.

1347.   Their name comes from the fact that they live in hedges and grunt like a pig.

1348.   Hedgehogs selectively hibernate.

1349.   They can easily kill snakes and are immune to venom.

1350.   They have dreadful eyesight and rely on hearing and smell.

Hippopotamuses

1351.   Hippos directly kill more humans than any other animal. Up to 5,000 people die every year from hippo attacks.

1352.   A hippo can hold its breath for 20 minutes.

1353.   "Hippopotamus" means "river horse" in Ancient Greek.

1354.   A male hippo can weigh 9,920lbs. That's nearly five tons.

1355.   A hippo's skin weighs a ton.

1356.   A hippo's skin is bulletproof.

1357.   They spend 16 hours submerged under water.

1358.   Hippos are vegetarian.

1359.   Hippos can't swim.

1360.   They travel six miles each night.

1361.   They eat 80lbs of grass a day.

1362.   A group of hippos is called a thunder or a bloat.

1363.   Baby hippos are born underwater.

1364.   The animal that is most related to the hippo is the dolphin.

1365.   Their roar is 115 decibels. That's louder than a motorcycle engine.

1366.   Their sweat is pink.

1367.   Hippos are 16.5ft long and 5ft 2 tall.

1368.   Despite their immense size, hippos can run up to 30mph. This means that a hippo can outrun Usain Bolt.

Horses

1369.   The triangular part of a horse's hoof is called a frog.

1370.   The fastest horse ever recorded could run at 43.97mph.

1371.   The smallest horse is a dwarf horse called Thumbelina. She is only 17 inches tall and weighs 57lbs.

1372.   Horses can sleep while standing.

1373.   Horses evolved from the Eohippus, which means "Dawn Horse." The Eohippus lived 60 million years ago. It weighed 12lbs and was 14 inches high.

1374.   "Horse" is derived from the Latin word "kurs," which means "to run."

1375.   All horses, ponies, and donkeys in the UK must have a passport.

1376.   The British army has more horses than tanks.

1377.   Alexander the Great had a horse called Bucephalus, which means "Ox Head."

1378.   Napoleon had a horse called Marengo.

1379.   Biologists gauge a horse's age from its teeth.

1380.   Horses live for 25-30 years.

1381.   Horses become visibly nervous when they smell blood.

1382.   The oldest horse ever was 62.

1383.   Horses have an incredible sense of smell and can use it to detect nervousness in a handler.

1384.   Their eyes can move independently.

1385.   Horses can differentiate between emotions in a human's voice.

1386.   There are 160 breeds of horse.

1387.   Hindus believe that Vishnu's final incarnation is of a white horse.

1388.   Horses only sleep for four hours a day.

1389.   The leader of a herd of horses can be male or female, which is rare in mammalian hierarchy.

1390.   Horses can't vomit.

1391.   A baby horse is called a foal. A young male horse is called a colt. A young female horse is called a filly.

1392.   A castrated male horse is called a gelding.

1393.   A male horse is called a stallion or a stud. A female horse is called a mare or a damn.

1394.   A group of horses is called a stable. A group of wild horses is called a band. A group of work horses is called a team. A group of colts is called a rag. A group of ponies is called a string. A group of racehorses is called a field.

1395.   The Arabian horse is the purest of all the breeds.

1396.   A horse's hoof is technically a single toe.

1397.   You can pay a licensed horse chiropractor to correct a horse's neck. Weirdly, this has been practiced since the 1890s. Although this sounds like a silly job, it's taken very seriously. It takes 220 hours of courses to earn a horse chiropractor license.

Hummingbirds

1398.   Hummingbirds have such a high metabolism rate, that they have to eat every few hours or they will starve to death.

1399.   The Sword-Billed Hummingbird is the only bird with a beak longer than its body.

1400.   Hummingbirds are the smallest type of birds.

1401.   The Ruby-Throated Hummingbird has to beat its wings 52 times a second to stay in the air.

1402.   The Bee Hummingbird has the smallest egg in the bird world, weighing 0.02oz. That's slightly heavier than a bumblebee.

1403.   Hummingbirds have less feathers than any other bird. Most of them have less than a thousand feathers.

1404.   Hummingbirds use small sticks and the silk from spider webs to weave nests.

1405.   Hummingbirds use hawks as bodyguards. They usually live under hawk nests to protect themselves from jays. Hawks stalk their prey from above, so jays avoid foraging below them, which creates a safety zone for the hummingbird.

Hyenas

1406.   A hyena laugh can be heard from three miles away.

1407.   A group of hyenas is called a cackle.

1408.   Hyenas laugh to indicate their age and social status.

1409.   Because of The Lion King, many people assume hyenas are stupid. In reality, hyenas are smarter than chimps. A study in Duke University showed that they perform better at problem-solving and social co-operation than chimpanzees. What's more interesting is that the hyenas performed the problems in silence, using non-verbal signals for communication.

1410.   The Lion King depicts hyenas as scavengers. Not only do hyenas hunt their prey and rarely scavenge, but lions are one of the biggest scavengers in the wild.

1411.   One thing that is depicted accurately in The Lion King is that hyenas and lions are interlocked in a war for territory and food. It doesn't help that they have the same prey. They steal each other's' food and kill each other's' cubs.

1412.   Female hyenas are more muscular and aggressive than their male counterparts. Each hyena group is ruled by a matriarch.

1413.   60% of hyena cubs die shortly after they're born.

1414.   Hyenas live for 25 years.

1415.   They can weigh up to 190lbs.

1416.   When a male Spotted Hyena reaches two years old, he will leave his cackle to find another. If he isn't welcome into his new cackle, he will be torn to shreds. If he is accepted, he will be harassed for the remainder of his life and will constantly struggle for food.

1417.   Ancient Egyptians domesticated hyenas for meat.

1418.   A cackle of hyenas can eat an entire zebra in under half an hour.

Insects

1419.   Insects have six legs and normally have wings. They have three main body parts; the head, the thorax, and the abdomen.

1420.   The first known insect was the Rhyniognatha hirsti. This 400-million-year old creature is also the first known animal that was capable of flight.

1421.   The first known animal to walk on land was a 1cm-long millipede called the Pneumodesmus. It is also the oldest air-breathing animal that we know of.

1422.   A centipede called the Scolopendra cataracta was discovered in June 2016. It is the only centipede in the world that can swim. It is 20cm long and highly venomous.

1423.   If you try to pick up a velvet worm, it will use its slime-cannon attack, which will drench you in 30cm of goo. The goo then solidifies, making it very difficult to move. The worm loses 10% of its body to accomplish this attack.

1424.   Fireflies are the only creatures that give off light without generating heat.

1425.   Fireflies are more efficient at producing light without wasting energy than any lightbulb in the world.

1426.   In 2013, scientists learned that the Issus insect is made of... gears.
   Not mechanical gears. Organic gears. These gears rotate to allow the insect to hop. This has never been seen in another animal.

1427. The Praying Mantis is the only insect that can turn its head.

1428. Ticks have eyes on their back.

1429. Limpets use their tongues like a jackhammer.

1430. 80% of all animals are insects.

1431. Earwigs have wings.

1432. A group of gnats is called a ghost.

1433. The Diania Cactiformis is a purple worm-like insect with jagged spikes protruding from every point of its body. It's nicknamed "The Walking Cactus."

Jaguars

1434.   Jaguars are 8ft long.

1435.   The jaguar has the strongest bite force of any big cat at 2,000lbs per square inch.

1436.   They live in Mexico, Brazil, and Argentina.

1437.   A group of jaguars is called a leap or a prowl.

1438.   They usually climb trees as a vantage point so they can pounce on their prey.

1439.   It's easy to get a leopard and a jaguar mixed up since they are big cats with black spots. However, a leopard's spots look like black circles. A jaguar's spots look like black roses. They are known as rosettes.

1440.   The word "jaguar" was a Native American term for any large carnivore. It could even be used to describe dogs.

Jellyfish

1441.   Jellyfish evaporate in the Sun since they are 97% water.

1442.   Their tentacles are made of thousands of cells known as cnidoblasts. These contain nematocysts, which contains a coiled stinging thread within. When a fish gets caught in a jellyfish's tentacles, the pressure inside the nematocysts forces the threads to uncoil like a spring-loaded harpoon.

1443.   Jellyfish are plankton from the phylum, Cnidaria, and the class, Scyphoza.

1444.   Since they are not fish, some aquariums have renamed them as jellies.

1445.   Their phylum name, Cnidaria, is Greek for "Stinging Nettle."

1446.   The class name, Scyphoza, is Greek for "Cup."

1447.   Jellyfish are genetically similar to coral.

1448.   The nematocysts in its tentacles are unique for every jellyfish in the world. Because of this, there is no universal remedy for jellyfish stings. Some sources say that urine or vinegar should be used on jellyfish stings. However, vinegar might work on one type of sting but may prove fatal to another.
    If you are stung by a jellyfish, get out of the water as soon as possible and wash the stung area with salt water to deactivate the stinging cells. Do NOT use fresh water as this will reactivate the sting. Remove the cells with a credit card and then wrap the area with a towel.
    If the stinging persists, you should go to hospital.

1449.   Jellyfish are made of six parts; the inner layer is the gastrodermis, which lines the gastrovascular cavity. The middle layer is the mesoglea. The outer layer is the epidermis. It also has an orifice and tentacles.

1450.   The Nomura Jellyfish weighs over 450lbs.

1451.   The Atolla Jellyfish glows when it is under attack.

1452.   One of the most famous jellyfish is said to be the Portuguese man-of-war. However, it's not actually a jellyfish. In fact, it's not even a single animal. It's a siphonophore; a colony of organisms that work in unity. It is made up of four separate polyps.

1453.   Jellyfish are the ocean's most efficient swimmers since they consume 48% less oxygen than any other swimming animal.

1454.   It has a short tube that hangs down from its body. It acts as a mouth and a digestive tract. In some species, the tube is surrounded by frilly pieces known as oral arms or mouth arms.

1455.   Jellyfish have been found in lakes and ponds.

1456.   Some jellyfish have tentacles that reach 200ft. That's as long as two blue whales.

1457.   Jellyfish can be up to 8ft in diameter.

1458.   A group of jellyfish is called a bloom, a brood, a fluther, a smack, or a smuth.

1459.   Its tentacles can sting you even if they are separated from its body.

1460.   A jellyfish has no brain, heart, ears, head, feet, legs, or bones.

However, jellyfish are technically alive because they have an elementary nervous system with receptors that detect light, vibrations, and chemicals.

1461.   The "head" of a jellyfish is known as the bell.

1462.   The Creeping Jellyfish is the smallest jellyfish in the world. Its bell is 0.5mm in diameter.

1463.   Jellyfish produce sexually, asexually, and hermaphroditically.

1464.   The Giant Jellyfish has only been spotted 17 times in the past century.

1465.   The Box Jellyfish (also known as the Sea Wasp or the Marine Stinger) has the most powerful sting in the animal kingdom. It can stop a person's heart within two minutes. Most people don't even realize they have been stung for the first 30 seconds.

1466.   A dead jellyfish can sting you.

1467.   Their predators include tuna, swordfish, turtles, and the pacific salmon.

1468.   The Immortal Jellyfish is the oldest creature on Earth. It can clone its cells so it can't die from old age. Some Immortal Jellyfish that are alive today could be 10,000 years old if not older.

1469.   Most jellyfish are carnivores and eat fish, fish eggs, crustaceans, and other jellyfish.

1470. The most common jellyfish in the US and Europe is the Moon Jellyfish.

1471. Jellyfish have existed for 650 million years.

1472. The Upside-Down Jellyfish doesn't float in water. Instead, it anchors itself to the ocean floor with its tentacles reaching upward.

1473. Crabs hitchhike on the bells of jellyfish.

1474. There are 2,000 species of jellyfish.

1475. Jellyfish are terrifying colonizers. Eight years after the Comb Jellyfish was introduced into the Black Sea in 1982, the collective mass of jellyfish weighed 900 million tons. It caused $350 million in losses to the Black Sea's fishing and tourism industries.

1476. Jellyfish are notoriously difficult to kill. Ocean pollution has led to 400 marine dead zones, which means nothing can survive there... except jellyfish.

1477. Jellyfish are one of the only animals that are not diminished by climate change, pollution, dams, and the overharvesting of fish. On the contrary, these factors have caused the jellyfish population to skyrocket.

1478. Only 70 jellyfish species can sting humans.

1479. Baby jellyfish are called polyps.

1480. A Japanese nuclear power plant had to be temporarily shut down after jellyfish stuck to its cooling system.

1481. In recent years, Japan got so sick of swimmers being stung by jellyfish, that they tried to exterminate them with a razor-wire net, shredding millions of them to pieces. However, a single jellyfish can give birth to 500 million polyps, each of which can grow to the size of a refrigerator.

Sadly, wiping out jellyfish is much harder than anyone imagined.

1482. Because jellyfish are so hard to see and can survive the crushing depths of the sea, scientists believe there could be as many as 300,000 different species of jellyfish yet to be discovered.

1483. Jellyfish are harvested for collagen, which is used for treating rheumatoid arthritis.

1484. In 2007, jellyfish killed 100,000 salmon in Northern Ireland, decimating the fishing industry.

1485. Although the Irukandji is only the size of a fingernail, its sting can kill a human.

1486. 10% of all captured marine life is jellyfish.

1487. An adult jellyfish is called a medusa. This is a reference to the Greek monster, Medusa the Gorgon, who had snakes for hair.

1488. 150 million people are stung by jellyfish every year.

1489. There is enough venom in a Box Jellyfish to kill 60 people.

1490. Many people assume that jellyfish move with their tentacles like an octopus. However, a jellyfish's tentacles are only used to catch and sting prey. Jellyfish move by taking in water through their bell and squirting it out, jettisoning them forward.

1491. Some jellyfish can see. They Box Jellyfish has 24 eyes; each of which can move independently of each other. This allows them to have 360-degree vision. Two of its eyes can see in color. To test its vision, researchers put jellyfish in a water tank and placed a white poll in the center. The jellyfish kept bumping into it.

The researchers then put a black pole in the center and the jellyfish kept dodging it.

Bizarrely, when the research team placed a red pole in the center, the jellyfish swam on the very edges of the aquarium.

1492. Box Jellyfish are technically not jellyfish. They belong to a class called cubozoans. True jellyfish have bowl-shaped bells while a box-jellyfish has a cube-shaped bell.

1493. The stingers from a jellyfish's tentacles shoot out faster than a bullet from a gun.

1494. Jellyfish can be green, purple, yellow, or red.

1495. Some jellyfish have stripes.

1496. If a fish is immune to a jellyfish sting, it will swim inside the jellyfish and then steer it around, using its body as a shield. If a predator tries to eat the fish, they will be stung by the jellyfish.

Kangaroos

1497.   Western Grey Kangaroos smell like curry.

1498.   Kangaroos box rival kangaroos to death.

1499.   The word "kangaroo" is derived from the Guugu Wimithirr word, "gangurru," which means "big foot."

1500.   There 40 species of kangaroo.

1501.   There's 23 million kangaroos in Australia.

1502.   A kangaroos is a marsupial, which means it has a pouch, where it keeps its young.

1503.   The biggest kangaroo is the Red Kangaroo. It's taller than a man and weighs about 190lbs. It's the largest marsupial in the world.

1504.   Kangaroos can run 40mph.

1505.   A baby kangaroo is called a joey and is only 2cm long when it is born.

1506.   A kangaroo's kick is strong enough to break a human's ribs.

1507.   Rapper, Vanilla Ice, has a pet kangaroo called Bucky Buckaroo.

1508.   A kangaroo can't jump unless its tail is touching the ground.

Koalas

1509.   Koala bears aren't related to bears. A koala is a marsupial, which means they have a pouch like a kangaroos.

1510.   They are excellent swimmers.

1511.   Koalas are facing extinction because over 50% of them have chlamydia.

1512.   A koala's brain is only 0.2% of body weight.

1513.   Before British settlers invaded Australia, there were 10 million koalas living in the wild. Now, there are only 43,000.

1514.   Koalas live for 18 years.

1515.   Poachers use the code words "Australian teddy bear" when referring to a koala bear.

1516.   They hug trees to cool off on hot days.

1517.   Koalas are the laziest animal in the world. They sleep for 22 hours a day.

1518.   Koalas have two thumbs on each paw.

1519.   Unless you're a forensic expert, koalas fingerprints are indistinguishable from human fingerprints.

Komodo Dragons

1520.   The komodo dragon was discovered by a WWI pilot that crashed into the lesser Sunda Islands. He thought the animal was a land crocodile.

1521.   Komodos are the world's largest lizards, measuring 10ft long.

1522.   These reptiles live in Indonesia.

1523.   They weigh 200lbs.

1524.   They live for over 30 years.

1525.   Komodo are cannibalistic.

1526.   They've been around for 3.5 million years.

1527.   They can use their tongue to locate a food source, even if it is three miles away.

1528.   Their tongue is forked.

1529.   Their teeth are serrated like a shark.

1530.   Komodo can't run and breathe at the same time.

1531.   They can see prey from 900ft away.

1532.   They can run 15mph.

1533.   The female lays 25 eggs at a time.

1534.   Komodos are good at climbing trees.

1535. They usually eat pigs, deer, snakes, fish, and buffalo.

1536. Unlike most animals, komodos eat bones and hooves.

1537. A komodo's bite is weaker than a cat's. If this reptile tries to bite down on something with too much force, it can crack open its skull.

Leeches

1538.   Leeches have 32 brains.

1539.   There are 650 known species of leeches.

1540.   Although the leech has a reputation as a blood-sucking worm, many of them are predators. They eat worms and fish.

1541.   20% of leeches live in the sea.

1542.   The largest leech is 18 inches long.

1543.   Although leeching was used to stop blood from clotting for centuries, they are still used today since there is no tool as efficient as a leech in preventing clotting. Leeches are efficient at dealing with plastic surgery, osteoarthritis, third-degree burns, and heavy bruising.

1544.   If a leech bites you, it's painless since it has its own anesthetic.

1545.   If a leech latches onto you, it's best not to tear it off as it can cut you badly. The best thing to do is to wait for it to have its fill. When a leech is full, it will simply drop off.

1546.   A leech can drink five times its own bodyweight.

1547.   Leeches have been used for medicinal purposes since 100B.C. in India.

1548.   In spite of the fact that a hippo has bulletproof skin, a leech's teeth are able to pierce through it.

Leopards

1549.   The Clouded Leopard doesn't roar like big cats, nor does it groom itself. It also has a unique resting position.

1550.   There are nine subspecies of leopard.

1551.   It is the smallest of the big cat family.

1552.   Despite its small size, the leopard is the strongest big cat pound for pound.

1553.   Leopards are the most elusive of the big cats. They are very difficult to track in the wild.

1554.   They are predominantly solitary animals.

1555.   Leopards are the only big cats that purr.

1556.   They eat gazelle, deer, monkeys, birds, rodents, and wildebeest.

1557.   Males are 50% larger than females.

1558.   They can be found in China, India, Malaysia, Russia, and most of Africa.

1559.   Leopards can leap more than 20ft.

1560.   Mother leopards give birth to six kittens at a time.

1561.   They can run 36mph.

1562.   They weigh 140lbs.

1563.   Leopards are known for dragging their prey into the branches of a tree to stop scavengers from stealing their meal.

1564.   The Clouded Leopard has the biggest canines proportion to its size in the entire animal kingdom. Their dagger-like teeth measure 1.8 inches.

Lions

1565.   The scientific name for a lion is Panthera leo. The lion belongs to the genus, Panthera, and is a member of the Felidae family. The other four members are the tiger, the jaguar, the leopard, and the snow leopard.

1566.   A white lion and a white tiger had four liger cubs in 2014. They are currently the rarest big cats in the world.

1567.   A lion's roar can be heard from five miles away.

1568.   Lionesses can have manes.

1569.   A group of lions is called a pride.

1570.   The Lion King was going to be called "King of the Jungle" until the Disney team realized that lions don't live in the jungle.

1571.   Male lions can weigh up to 550lbs.

1572.   In the wild, lions live for up to 14 years.

1573.   The lion on the MGM symbol is called Leo. He was first used in 1929.

1574.   Five different lions have been used for the MGM symbol.

1575.   Below the lion on MGM is the motto, "Ars Gratia Artis," which means "Art for Art's Sake."

1576.   The lion is the national animal of Albania, Belgium, Bulgaria, England, Ethiopia, Luxembourg, the Netherlands, and Singapore.

1577. If a male leopard and a lioness mate, she will give birth to a leopon.

1578. A lioness and a male jaguar can have an offspring known as a jaglion.

1579. Half of a lion's diet is from scavenging.

1580. Male lions can mate up to 40 times a day.

1581. Lionesses do 90% of the hunting. In spite of this, the male lion has first dibs on eating the caught prey and are allowed to eat as much as they want. Sometimes, male lions eat all of the carcass and leave nothing for his mate or cubs.

1582. Some male lions sleep for up to 22 hours a day.

1583. In the wild, lions make about 20 kills a year.

1584. A lion's mane gets darker as he gets older. Lions with dark manes are considered to be very attractive to lionesses.

1585. A lion can leap as far as 36ft.

1586. Most lions get kicked out of their pride by the age of two in an attempt to establish dominance. Because of this, 12% of lions die before adulthood.

1587. It is the only member of the cat family to have a tasseled tail. The tassel can give signals like "come over here" or "stay away from me."

1588. Lions eat about 17lbs of meat a day. That would be like a human eating 70 burgers.

1589. Lions are excellent swimmers.

1590. Lions aren't good at moving their eyes so they have to turn their entire head to look around.

1591. About 100 people are killed by lions ever year.

1592. Lions are 10ft long.

1593. Tanzania has more lions than any other country.

1594. White lions in Africa are seen as a symbol of peace and prosperity.

1595. Lions have the weakest bite in the big cat family, measuring 600lbs per square inch. That's nearly 10 times weaker than a crocodile.

1596. A lion can see six times better in the dark than a human.

1597. Lions can run up to 50mph.

1598. The two stone lions that stand outside New York Public library are called Patience and Fortitude. They were named in the 1930s to represent the qualities New Yorkers exhibited during the Great Depression.

1599. Lions are the only big cats where the males and females look drastically different.

1600. Male lions have two jobs; mate with as many females as possible and protect the pride from invading lions.

1601.   An average male lion maintains their pride for four years.

1602.   A lion's pride territory can stretch up to 100 square miles.

1603.   Male lions mate only for a few seconds.

1604.   Friedrich Nietzsche (who coined the phrase, "What doesn't kill you makes you stronger.") wrote Thus Spoke Zarathustra. In the book, he uses a lion to symbolise rebellion against traditional knowledge to form a new morality. He called people who think this way "Ubermensch" which translates into "Superman." Struggling writers, Jerry Siegel and Joe Shuster, loved this name and used it for their superhero in Action Comics #1 in 1938.
        So all comic books exist... because of a lion.

1605.   The lion is the most social big cat.

1606.   A lioness will often bring small animals alive to her cubs so they can practice their hunting skills.

1607.   Lions begin to roar when they are two.

1608.   Lions can be tan, brown, yellow, black, and even red.

1609.   A pride is usually made up of 13 lions but can be as little as two or as many as 40.

1610.   There are two species of lion – African and Asian. There are six subspecies of African lions.

1611.   A lion's mane starts to grow at 18 months and has fully grown when the lion is five years old.

1612.   Lionesses usually spend their entire lives in the same pride that they were born in. Lionesses are rarely welcomed into new prides and usually don't live very long.

1613.   Lions have unique whiskerprints, similar to how humans have fingerprints.

1614.   A lion can open its jaws up to 1ft. That's larger than a human head.

1615.   They have a scent gland in-between their toes. When they scratch trees to sharpen their claws, they also mark the tree as their territory.

1616.   Lions can hear prey up to a mile away.

1617.   The oldest image of a lion dates back 32,000 years. It was found in the Chauvet Cave in southern France.

1618.   Apart from humans, buffalos kill lions more than any other animal.

1619.   Lions can travel 12 miles in a single day.

1620.   In Ancient Rome, criminals would be fed to the lions. This was called "Damnatio as bestias," which is Latin for "damnation to the beasts."

1621.   The Griffin is a mythical creature with the body of a lion and the head and wings of an eagle. It represents the Sun, wisdom, vengeance, strength, and salvation. It is also the animal that represents the house of Gryffindor in the Harry Potter series.

1622.   When a lion is attacking its prey, the victim will instinctively kick the lion's belly. However, a lion's belly is so loose, that it can be kicked full force without hurting the lion at all.

1623.   Killing a lion can utterly destroy a pride. Poachers will naturally kill the alpha lion because it's the biggest species of cat.

However, when the pride's leader is killed, it destabilises the whole group. On top of that, killing the leader wipes out the genes of the largest and healthiest male.

1624.   2,000 years ago, there were over a million lions. In the 1940s, there was only 450,000. Nowadays, there are only 32,000 in the world.

Lizards

1625.   There are over 6,000 lizard species.

1626.   Lizards are reptiles with overlapping scales. The only reptiles that have overlapping scales but wouldn't be classified as lizards would be tuataras and snakes.

1627.   Some reptiles have slimy skin. Lizards nearly always have a cool and dry exterior.

1628.   The Jesus Christ Lizard is so light, that it can run on water for a few seconds.

1629.   The Whiptail Lizard is an all-female species. They have evolved so their eggs hatch unfertilized so males don't need to exist.

1630.   Most lizards have a weak tail that breaks off when ensnared by a predator, allowing the lizard to escape. The tail will grow back over time.

1631.   If a lizard loses a limb, it will regenerate.

1632.   Lizards smell by licking the air.

1633.   Although many lizards are venomous, most of them are harmless to humans.

1634.   Some lizards such as the Basilisk or the Collared Lizard can run on its hind legs.

1635.   The Flying Lizard can glide from tree to tree.

1636.   The only dangerous lizards are Komodo Dragons, the Gila Monster, and the Mexican Beaded Lizard.

1637.   Some lizards can spew blood from their eyes.

1638.   They enjoy basking in the sunlight.

1639.   The largest class of lizards are skinks. There are over 1,300 types of skinks in the world.

1640.   Skinks used to lay eggs but now they give birth.

1641.   They conserve water by excreting salt.

1642.   The gecko is the only lizard with vocal cords.

1643.   Lizards have been around for 200 million years and used to be as large as dinosaurs.

1644.   Lizards never stop growing. They shed their skin when they need to grow more.

1645.   The Sandfish is a skink lizard that lives in the desert. It is known as the Sandfish since it can literally swim through sand. This allows it to move through the desert at rapid speed but saves it from the Sun's rays by being under the sand rather than on top of it.

Llamas

1646.   The scientific name for a llama is "lama glama."

1647.   Llamas are related to camels and are part of the camelid family. Camelids have existed for 40 million years. Llamas have existed for three million years.

1648.   Llamas spit when they are irritated.

1649.   Llamas were domesticated about 4,500 years ago.

1650.   Llamas can weigh up to 450lbs.

1651.   A llama can carry 25% of its body weight on a 10-mile trek.

1652.   Llamas are vegetarians.

1653.   The stomach of a llama has three departments – the rumen, the masum, and the abomasum.

1654.   Llamas have two wild cousins called the vicuna and the guanaco. They have never been domesticated.

Lobsters

1655.   A lobster's brain is in its throat, its nervous system is in its abdomen, its teeth are in its stomach, and its kidneys are in its head.

1656.   Slaves used to eat lobsters. As a result, the animal was associated with poverty until the 20th century.

1657.   Lobsters can cost $40 (£30) to eat. However, they were so abundant during the 18th and 19th century, that they were fed to pigs, used as bait to catch other fish, and their shells were used as fertilizer. Lobsters were so popular in North America that they would wash ashore in piles up to 2ft high.

1658.   In Iceland, lobsters are so common, they cost $4 (£3.)

1659.   Live lobsters are never red. They are only red after they are cooked. When they are alive, they can be yellow, blue, orange, or white.

1660.   Lobsters can shed a claw, leg, or antennae if it becomes trapped in the teeth or claws of a predator. The organ will eventually regenerate.

1661.   No lobster has ever been found that died of old age.

1662.   Lobsters never stop growing until the day they die. Also, their shell gets harder as they get older.

1663.   Lobster fishermen only collect medium-sized lobsters. If the lobster is too big, it doesn't taste as nice. In Maine, a lobster's body must be at least 3.25 inches but can't be more than 5 inches.

1664.   Lobsters shed their shells.

1665.   A female can only mate after she's shed her shell.

1666.   When they are scared, lobsters swim backwards by rapidly curling and uncurling their tails.

1667.   When they can't find food, lobsters resort to cannibalism.

1668.   Their eggs are called roe.

1669.   They feed on bottom dwellers like clams, snails, and crabs.

1670.   Its left claw is called the pincer and its right claw is called the crusher.

1671.   Native Americans used to eat lobsters by wrapping them in seaweed.

1672.   Lobsters are filled with protein, providing 28g per cup. That's half the amount of protein a human adult should eat a day. Also, they only have 96 calories and 2g of fat.

1673.   Soft-shell lobsters taste sweeter. Soft-shells are often known as shedders.

1674.   They have poor eyesight and rely on their sense of smell and taste.

1675.   Lobsters have clear blood. When cooked, their blood turns into a whitish gel.

1676.   They drown in fresh water.

1677.   The black line on the lobster's tail are unfertilized eggs.

1678.   Their claws exert pressure of up to 100lbs per square inch. That's strong enough to break a person's finger.

1679.   Lobsters are nocturnal.

1680.   Lobstermen start work at 4:30am.

1681.   Lobsters will carry their eggs for up to a year.

1682.   0.1% of lobster eggs will live longer than six weeks.

1683.   Their shells were once used to make golf balls.

1684.   Lobsters can be two-toned. This means that one side of it can be blue and the other side of it can be black.

1685.   If you turn this crustacean on its head by using its claws to balance it and then rub the top of its tail, it will do a handstand for several hours. Some chefs do this to keep the lobster still while they cut it open.

1686.   Lobster fishing is a huge industry in Maine and is home to 6,000 licensed lobstermen. When a new person applies for a license, they usually can't start until one of the lobstermen retires because there is simply too many of them. Lobstermen get paid about $50,000 a year. Although this sounds like a lot, they need to catch 150lbs of lobster a day to cover the cost of bait and gas.

Mammals

1687.   There are over 4,000 species of mammal.

1688.   A mammal is an animal with fur that provides milk for its young. Although mammals are considered to be animals that produce live young, the platypus and the pangolin lay eggs but are classified as mammals.

1689.   Almost all mammals (including humans) take the same length of time to urinate – 21 seconds.

1690.   A beaver-like animal called the kimbetopsalis was discovered recently and is said to be one of the earliest mammals ever found. Although it went extinct millions of years ago, it seemed to survive the cataclysm that ended the dinosaurs.

1691.   The zorilla is the world's smelliest animal. Unsurprisingly, it's related to the skunk. Its stench is said to smell like rotten eggs inside a gym locker. It can be smelt from a mile away.

1692.   Binturongs (bearcats) smell like buttered popcorn.

1693.   A group of badgers is called a cete.

1694.   A porcupine can fight off a pride of lions.

1695.   A seal can use its whiskers to feel a submarine from 130ft away.

1696.   The honey badger is the most ferocious animal in the world. It can eat porcupines, poisonous snakes, raid beehives, kidnap baby cheetahs, and steal food from lions. It will not back down from a fight from any animal and it will always attack the genitalia of an animal first.

1697.   The first known mammal was the Hadrocodium Wui. This 1.5-inch-long creature bears a resemblance to a mouse.

Mammoths

1698.   The first known musical instrument was a flute made out of mammoth ivory.

1699.   The Imperial Mammoth was twice the size of the African Elephant.

1700.   Researchers can tell what time of the year a mammoth died in by examining its tusks.

1701.   Some mammoths were very small. The Cretan Dwarf Mammoth was only 3.4ft tall.

1702.   Harvard geneticists have successfully spliced wooly mammoth DNA into living cells from an Asian Elephant. Although a fully cloned mammoth is a long way away, hopefully an elephant with mammoth DNA should be born in our lifetime.

1703.   Thanks to global warming, more and more frozen mammoths have been discovered.

1704.   A pair of mammoth tusks is worth about $80,000.

1705.   Mammoths went extinct in 2600B.C. which was the same time the Pyramids of Giza were being built.

Manatees

1706.   When Christopher Columbus made his journey to America, he claimed to have seen mermaids. They were actually manatees.

1707.   Although manatees resemble hippos, seals, and walruses, they are mostly related to elephants.

1708.   The largest manatee was the Steller's Sea Cow. It was 10 meters long and weighed about 12 tons. It was discovered in 1741. Because its fat was valuable for creating oil and butter, fishermen hunted it to extinction. Within 27 years of its discovery, the Stellar Sea Cow was wiped out.

1709.   It is illegal to kill a manatee. Weirdly, it's also illegal to hug a manatee.

1710.   A manatee has the smallest brain among mammals compared to its body size. This means that the manatee is probably the least intelligent mammal in the world.

1711.   A painting of a manatee from 5,000 years ago can be seen in Tambun Cave in Malaysia.

1712.   Manatees belong to the Sirenian family.

1713.   A dugong is a relative of the manatee. It is the only marine herbivorous mammal. Although many sources say that manatees are herbivores, they do eat fish from time to time.

1714.   Dugongs are mentioned in the Bible.

1715.   Dugongs used to appear in sideshows as mermaids.

Meerkats

1716. Meerkats are mammals and are related to mongooses.

1717. They can also be called suricates.

1718. It is the only animal in the mongoose family that doesn't have a bushy tail.

1719. Meerkats live in Botswana, Namibia, Angola, and South Africa.

1720. A group of meerkats is called a mob, gang, or clan.

1721. A mob usually contains 20 meerkats but can have as many as 50.

1722. They normally live 7-10 years in the wild. They usually live for 13 years while in captivity.

1723. Adult meerkats are about 1ft tall.

1724. They eat insects, lizards, snakes, scorpions, spiders, plants, eggs, mushrooms, centipedes, and mice.

1725. They are immune to several types of snake venom.

1726. A meerkat can easily spot a predator from 300 meters away.

1727. A mob always has one sentry on lookout for predators while the others look for food.

1728. A meerkat uses its tail to stand upright.

1729.   They usually stand up in the morning to absorb heat on their bellies.

1730.   When a meerkat spots a predator, it will bark and whistle to alert the rest of the mob.

Mice

1731. Mice are part of the Muroidea family, which includes hamsters, gerbils, and rats.

1732. White mice are chosen for experiments because it's easy to find their veins.

1733. They live for one or two years.

1734. A group of mice is called a mischief.

1735. Mice have 225 bones, which means that they have more bones than a human.

1736. Contrary to what Tom & Jerry have been telling us for years, mice don't like cheese.

1737. Mice use their whiskers to sense smooth and rough surfaces. They are also used to gauge temperature changes.

1738. Mice and human DNA are 97.5% identical.

1739. Like all rodents, a mouse's teeth never stop growing.

1740. Mice explore their territory daily and do not like any foreign object.

1741. Mice can produce eight litters of 16 babies (called pinkies) a year. That's 128 babies a year.

1742. Mice make facial expressions to communicate to other mice.

1743. Mice can produce 80 droppings per day.

1744.   Despite the fact that all medical experiments are done on mice, only 20% of the test results can be replicated for humans.

1745.   Mice are very protective of their home and will rarely venture further than eight meters from their nest.

1746.   They can jump down four meters without hurting themselves.

1747.   The Scorpion Mouse is the only mouse that is carnivorous. It's immune to venom and howls like a wolf.

Miscellaneous

1748.   An herbivore is an animal that only eats plants.

1749.   A carnivore is an animal that only eats meat.

1750.   An omnivore eats plants and meat.

1751.   Carnivores usually sweat through their mouths.
Herbivores tend to sweat through their skin.

1752.   A rodent is a mammal with incisor teeth that never
stop growing.

1753.   A herd of unicorns is called a blessing.

1754.   The film, Babe, required over 1,000 animal
trainers.

1755.   A vertebrate is an animal that has a backbone.
Insects, crabs, lobsters, clams, octopi, starfish, worms,
and snails don't have backbones so they would be
classified as invertebrates.

1756.   There are 173,000 venomous species on Earth.

1757.   Animals had welfare rights in the US before
children did.

1758.   Animals react to social pressure just like humans.

1759.   70% of jungle animals rely on figs.

1760.   Pope Paul VI said that animals go to heaven.

1761.   The Moray Eel is one of the weirdest animals in
the world. It holds its prey with its curved teeth. Then, it

uses a second set of jaws in its throat to pull it inside. The eel evolved this way because it can't create a vacuum to swallow its food like other fish.

That's right. It has two sets of jaws!

1762. The last animal in the dictionary is a tropical weevil called the Zyzzyva.

1763. 9% of pet owners have birthday parties for pets.

1764. The Amazon rainforest consist of 2,220 species of fish, 1,200 species of bird, 420 species of mammal, 420 species of amphibian, and 370 species of reptile. This means that 10% of the world's known species live in the Amazon rainforest.

1765. In China, cosmetic products have to be tested on animals before being tested on humans.

1766. An average meat-eating person consumes about 7,000 animals in their lifetime.

1767. Dogs, cows, bulls, sheep, and dolphins can commit suicide.

1768. Zoophobia is a fear of animals.

1769. Agrizoophobia is a fear of wild animals.

1770. The naked mole-rat is immune to cancer and its cells are studied by scientists and biologists in an attempt to harness its immunity to kill diseases.

1771. Some animals are remarkable at regenerating themselves. If a starfish is cut in half, it can form into two starfish. But the animal with the greatest regenerating abilities is the flatworm. Its healing powers are so vast; it can regrow into an individual creature 1/279th of its original size. That means if you chopped it into 279 pieces, each piece could hypothetically heal fully and live as 279 separate animals.

1772.   There are English 40 words for cougar including mountain lion, puma, panther, catamount, and Florida panther. It holds the Guinness record for the animal with the greatest number of names.

1773.   Everyone knows that rodents are a nuisance. In fact, some rodents like the prairie dog are considered such a nuisance, that you can make a living removing them from an area. Professional prairie dog removers can earn up to $100 for each prairie dog removed.

1774.   During WWII, workers at a London zoo killed all of their venomous animals just in case the zoo was bombed and the animals escaped.

1775.   The Guinness World Records stopped awarding fat animals in an attempt to discourage deliberate overfeeding.

1776.   The Phyllodesmium acanthorhinum is one of the most beautiful animals in the world. It's a solar powered sea slug that glows in the dark.

1777.   Scientists discover 41 new species every day.

1778.   The two-toed sloth is not genetically related to the three-toed sloth. This is known as convergent evolution – when two animals look almost identical but have no genetica connection.

1779.   Sharks, chickens, snakes, and komodo dragons

can have virgin births. The process is known as parthenogenesis.

1780. Sea-sponges, starfish, tapeworms, jellyfish, crayfish, boa constrictors, whiptail lizards, gall wasps, komodo dragons, aphids, and hammerhead sharks can clone themselves.

1781. There are 500 trillion Antarctic krill on Earth, making it the world's most abundant animal. That means there's approximately 65,800 Antarctic krill for every human.

1782. Prairie dogs live in "towns." The largest town ever found was over 40,000 miles and was inhabited by 400,000 prairie dogs.

1783. No new animals have been domesticated in the last 4,000 years.

1784. You should never punish a pet for doing something wrong. They can't make the connection between the wrongdoing and the punishment. If you constantly shout at your pet aggressively, they'll just assume that you're not nice, and will become more likely to misbehave in the future. The best thing to do is treat them when they behave.

1785. The Ophiacodon snyapsid is the first recorded animal to be warm-blooded.

1786. Panama has the most diverse wild life in all of Central Africa. In 1980, scientists studied 19 trees in the tropics and found 1,200 beetles. Of the 1,200 insects, 960 species had never been found anywhere on Earth! The World Resources Institute says that scientists probably have a better understanding of how many stars there are in the galaxy than how many species there are on Earth.

Moles

1787.   A mole can triangulate an odor's position within seconds. Basically, they smell in stereo. It is the only mammal that possesses this ability.

1788.   Many people believe moles have no eyes. Although it's very difficult to see their eyes, moles can see, although very poorly. Their tiny eyes prevent them from being clogged up with dirt while they burrow underground.

1789.   Some moles are aquatic.

1790.   There are 20 species of mole.

1791.   They mainly eat insects.

1792.   Moles are usually about 0.5ft long.

1793.   Their saliva paralyses worms and insects.

1794.   Moles stay in their tunnels in the day and venture out at night.

1795.   A mole has twice as much blood as other mammals proportioned to its size. This allows it to have enough oxygenated blood to breathe while its underground.

1796.   Moles are among the few mammals that don't hibernate.

1797.   Their main predator is the owl.

1798.   A mole can dig 300ft in one night.

Mollusks

1799.   Although there are many types of mollusks, everyone will be familiar with two types – gastropods and cephalopods. Gastropods have a slimy texture and have a shell e.g. snail, clam, oyster, etc.

Cephalopods are tentacle mollusks with a large head and tentacles e.g. squid, octopus.

Mollusks are invertebrates, which means they don't have bones.

1800.   There are 85,000 species of mollusks.

1801.   23% of all marine species are mollusks.

1802.   The scientific study of mollusks is called malacology.

1803.   There are 60,000 species of snails and slugs.

1804.   Malacologists can't decide how many subclasses of mollusks there are. Some say there are eight while others say that there are 10.

1805.   Mollusks have an abundant amount of calcium in their bodies.

1806.   The word "mollusk" is derived from the Latin word "molluscus," which means "soft."

1807.   Sea Hares are mollusks that live under the sea. Although they are extremely slow and incapable of putting up a fight, they have a very unique way to combat predators; they shoot a purple ink called opaline, which makes other animals incapable of using their sense of smell, making the Sea Hare almost invisible to potential predators.

Monkeys

1808.   The word "monkey" is derived from the Dutch word "manneken," which means "little man."

1809.   There are three kinds of primates – apes, Old World monkeys, and New World monkeys.

1810.   Unlike Old World monkeys, New World monkeys have prehensile tails. Prehensile tails help monkeys grasp objects, swing, and balance themselves on branches.

1811.   A monkey is any primate that is not a human, prosimian, or an ape. Also, unlike apes, monkeys have tails.

1812.   There are 50 million monkeys in the world.

1813.   Apes and Spider Monkeys swing arm-to-arm in trees. However, monkeyS usually run across branches.

1814.   The Black-Fronted Titi (which is brown) is a monkey that can be found in Brazil. It is the only animal on Earth apart from humans that understands syntax. This means that it can string certain sounds together to form a sentence.

Although dolphins are the world's smartest animals apart from humans, their communication is simple; they use one sound for food, one sound for a threat, one sound if they see something interesting, etc.

However, a Black-Fronted Titi can form a sentence that is the equivalent of "there are predatory cats near the feet of the trees."

Some scientists were skeptical that the Titi was this clever so they tried to fool a group of them by hurling a leopard teddy into their habitat. The Titi instantly adapted new calls for the teddy.

1815.   Crystal the Capuchin has starred in many movies including The Hangover: Part 2, and Night at the Museum. She was given a Life Time Diva Achievement at the sixth annual American Humane Society awards for animal actors (aka the Pawscars.) She collected her award wearing a dress and a necklace.

1816.   The largest monkey is the Mandrill, measuring 3.3ft. It's easy to identity due to its red-and-blue snout.

1817.   In The Lion King, the mentor, Rafiki, is a Mandrill.

1818.   Monkeys show aggression by grinning or yawning.

1819.   The smallest monkey is the Pygmy Marmoset. It measured 12cm and weighs 85g.

1820.   The Three Wise Monkeys is a Japanese concept that embodies the proverbial principal, "See no evil, hear no evil, speak no evil." Mizaru covers his eyes, Kikazaru covers his ears, and Iwazaru covers his mouth. Outside of Japan, the moneys are usually known as Mizaru, Mikazaru, and Mazaru.
        The Western equivalent of this proverb is, "Turning a blind eye."

1821.   Monkeys have the most colorful faces in the mammalian kingdom.

1822.   Monkeys can carry tuberculosis, hepatitis, and herpes.

1823.   10 New World monkey species are nocturnal. All

Old World monkeys sleep at night.

1824.   There are 96 species of Old World monkeys.

1825.   There are 81 species of New World monkeys.

1826.   Capuchins and Squirrel Monkeys are the only New World monkeys with opposable thumbs.

1827.   Old World monkeys are divided into two subfamilies; generalists and specialists. Generalists eat almost anything. Specialists mainly eat leaves.

1828.   A Howler scream can be heard two miles away, making them the loudest monkeys in the world.

1829.   Capuchins are extremely intelligent. They smash nuts open with rocks, insert branches into narrow areas to capture food, remove spikes from thorny plants by rubbing them against a branch, protect their hands from sharp objects by covering them with leaves, and use large branches to whack snakes.

Mosquitoes

1830.   Mosquitoes are insects that drink blood from animals including humans. While mosquitoes drink the blood, a plasmodium parasite that lives in mosquitoes can be transferred to the human's bloodstream. Doing so causes an infectious disease called malaria. Symptoms usually develop 10-15 days after being bitten. If it is not treated, the disease can become fatal. This leads to one million deaths annually. Mosquitoes kill more humans that any other animal by far. The second-biggest killer is the hippo but they only manage to kill 5,000 humans annually.

1831.   600 million people are infected with malaria every year.

1832.   Mosquitoes were the biggest cause of death until very recently since precautions have been taken to prevent malaria. Nowadays, the biggest cause of death is smoking.

1833.   The deadliest mosquito is the Anopheles.

1834.   Mosquitoes prefer to drink from people with type O blood.

1835.   Buzzing mosquitoes don't cause malaria. It's the silent ones you have to watch out for.

1836.   Only females drink blood.

1837.   Malaria rapidly weakens the body, causing the immune system to shut down, which enables other diseases to invade the body.

1838.   Malaria is more common in pregnant women.

Pregnant women lose all immunity to the disease.

1839.   It takes five years for a person to build up the antibodies needed to resist malaria. If a child under the age of five gets infected, it is far less likely he or she will recover.

1840.   Malaria causes an infected person to develop a body temperature of 104 degrees Celsius. That is the same temperature that sperm cooks at. This means that if a man gets infected with malaria, he can become infertile.

1841.   Mosquitoes can smell humans far better at night.

1842.   Half of every human in history has died from malaria.

1843.   It was only common knowledge that mosquitoes cause malaria in the 1930s.

1844.   Mosquitos have existed for over 100 million years and used to suck blood from dinosaurs.

1845.   There are 3,500 species of mosquitoes worldwide.

1846.   "Mosquito" is Spanish for "little fly."

1847.   It would take 1.2 million mosquitoes to suck a human dry.

1848.   A mosquito can drink three times its weight in blood.

1849.   They can lay 300 eggs at a time.

1850.   Mosquitoes spend their first 10 days in water.

1851.   Mosquitoes live for two months.

1852.   Males can locate females by the sound of their wings.

1853.   Mosquitoes can only fly 1.5mph.

1854.   They normally stay a few 100ft from wherever they hatched.

1855.   Mosquitoes can only fly up to three miles at a time.

1856.   Mosquitoes choose their victims based on their smell. Human skin produces 340 chemical odors and will smell more prominent to a mosquito if the person is sweating.

1857.   Mosquitoes can hear a human's blood.

1858.   Many people worried that mosquitoes could spread AIDS by drinking the blood of an AIDS victim and then passing it on to another person. Luckily, if a mosquito drinks from an AIDS carrier, the insect expunges the disease.

1859.   Alexander the Great is believed to have died from malaria.

1860.   Bug zappers are useless against mosquitoes. Other electronic repellers have proven ineffective against these insects.

1861.   Although bats kill more insects than any other creature, very few of them kill mosquitoes.

1862.   There are 176 species in the US.

1863.   The bigger you are, the more likely that a mosquito will target you.

1864.   Athletic people produce more CO_2 and lactic acid, which a mosquito can detect from 75ft.

1865.   Mosquitoes are attracted to people with smelly feet.

1866.   Mosquitoes numbers go up by 500% during a full Moon.

1867.   For some reason, mosquitoes are attracted to Limburger cheese.

1868.   Male mosquitoes only eat flower nectar.

1869.   Some mosquitoes only drink from amphibians and birds.

1870.   Their wings can beat up to 600 times per second.

1871.   Salt Marsh mosquitoes can travel up to 100 miles for a meal.

1872.   All mosquitoes rely on water to breed.

1873.   Japanese scientists studied the anatomy of mosquitoes to create a painless hypodermic needle.

1874.   Malaria is the only cure for syphilis.

<u>Moths</u>

1875.   There are 200,000 species of moths.

1876.   There are 11,000 species of moth in the US.

1877.   The Pink Underwing Moth looks like a human skull.

1878.   Many people assume moths look like duller version of butterflies. However, some moths look like wasps or hummingbirds.

1879.   The Atlas Moth scares predators by folding its wings so it looks like two snakes.

1880.   Contrary to popular belief, moths aren't attracted to fire or lightbulbs. The light disorients them and they might go closer to the light out of confusion rather than curiosity.

1881.   Moths don't eat clothes. Their larvae do.

1882.   Moths can mimic other animals to draw them in before killing them.

1883.   Although some moths are pests, others pollinate flowers.

1884.   A male can smell a female from seven miles away.

1885.   They smell with their antennae.

1886.   Tiger Moths use clicking sounds to jam bat sonar, preventing bats from eating them.

1887.   Some moths never eat throughout their entire
lives. They survive on the energy stored in their bodies
as caterpillars.

<u>Octopi</u>

1888. It's illegal to perform surgery on an octopus without anesthetic.

1889. There are 300 species of octopus.

1890. Octopi use bits of wood to pry open clam shells.

1891. They have rectangular pupils.

1892. Sometimes, an octopus will tap on its prey in one direction, knowing it will instinctively try to escape in the other direction. However, the octopus will already have its other tentacle ready to snatch it.

1893. A baby octopus is about 2mm tall.

1894. Octopi have been around for at least 296 million years.

1895. Octopus wrestling was a popular sport during the 1960s.

1896. Octopi don't have eight arms. They have six arms and two legs.

1897. Octopi hold grudges and will spit ink at humans that they don't like.

1898. An octopus can make its way through a maze faster than a human.

1899. A group of octopi is called a consortium.

1900. An octopus can unscrew a childproof jar.

1901.   The Blue-Ringed Octopus is the deadliest octopus in the world. Its bite is nearly always fatal and there is no anti-venom.

1902.   Some octopi only live for six months.

1903.   If an octopus is starving, it will eat its own arms.

1904.   The Land-Walking Octopus is the only one of its species to crawl on land.

1905.   An octopus' grip is so strong, very few humans would have the strength to remove one.

1906.   An octopus' brain is spread out across its body. It has a central brain in the head, backup brains in each tentacle, and another behind its eyes.

1907.   If an octopus loses a tentacle, the tentacle's backup brain will activate and it will be able to move by itself.

1908.   Most animals can only learn through first-hand experience. However, octopi can learn to climb, get around an obstacle, or escape from a tank if they see another animal do it.

1909.   An average sized octopus can escape through a 1cm hole.

1910.   Octopi have three hearts.

1911.   Octopi have a freakishly good memory.

1912.   An octopus' testicles are in its head.

1913.   The Giant Pacific Octopus gives birth to 50,000 babies. Only a handful survive.

1914.   Octopi have been increasing in number over the last 60 years due to global warming.

1915.   An octopus' suction cups can taste whatever it touches.

1916.   Only two six-limbed octopi have ever been recorded.

1917.   The female Blanket Octopus is 40,000 times larger than the male. It is the largest gender size difference in the animal kingdom. Because of this, a male Blanket Octopus was only discovered in 2002.

1918.   The Indonesian Mimic Octopus can change its colours and drastically change its shape so it looks like predators like a Sea Snake or a Lion Fish.

1919.   Despite the fact octopi move elegantly, there is no rhythm to their movements, which is quite rare in the animal kingdom.

1920.   The biggest octopus ever weighed 156lbs.

1921.   Octopi kill sharks.

1922.   An octopus called Inky escaped from the Nat'l Aquarium in New Zealand by sliding out of a small opening, crawling through the floor, and squeezing through a pipe that lead to the ocean.

Orangutans

1923. Orangutans are red apes with arms that are longer than their entire bodies.

1924. If an orangutan spreads its arms out, it would be 7ft wide.

1925. They spend up to 90% of their time in trees.

1926. "Orangutan" is a Malay word which means "man of the forest."

1927. They are mostly found in Indonesia and Malaysia.

1928. There are three subspecies of orangutan. It is only possible to tell the difference between them by using DNA testing.

1929. They live for up to 40 years. Captive orangutans can live for nearly 60 years.

1930. They can weigh up to 180lbs.

1931. They are usually between 4-5ft tall.

1932. Their call can be heard from 1.2 miles away.

1933. It's not uncommon for males to have beards and moustaches.

1934. They eat durian fruits, flowers, honey, bark, leaves, and insects.

1935. Unlike other apes, orangutans like to live alone.

1936. They use sticks to pull honey out of beehives.

1937.   Females normally have one or two babies at a time. They live with their mother until they are six or seven years old.

1938.   100 years ago, there were about 315,000 orangutans in the wild. Now, there are less than 70,000.

1939.   Orangutans like to eat soap. For some reason, the ape has no difficulty digesting it.

1940.   Orangutans make umbrellas out of leaves when it rains.

Ostriches

1941.   An ostrich's brain is smaller than its eyes.

1942.   The ostrich is the largest bird, measuring up to 6ft 7. However, some ostriches can be as tall as 9ft.

1943.   The ostrich is the only bird that willingly looks after other females' eggs.

1944.   Ostriches can run 43mph.

1945.   The ostrich is the fastest bird in the world that can't fly.

1946.   Ostriches can live for up to 40 years.

1947.   Male ostriches roar like a lion.

1948.   The ostrich eats fruit, shrubs, flowers, seeds, and locusts.

1949.   It lives in groups of 5-50 birds.

1950.   They can weigh up to 245lbs.

1951.   "Struthious" means "ostrich-like."

1952.   Ostriches don't have teeth so they have to swallow pebbles to pulverize food in their stomachs.

1953.   Despite what many sources say, ostriches don't bury their heads in the sand.

1954.   The ostrich lays the largest egg in the bird world, weighing 3lbs.

1955.   Despite the ostrich egg's size, it is the smallest bird egg proportioned to the bird's size.

1956.   Ostriches have three stomachs.

1957.   Most ostriches live in Africa and South of Sahara.

1958.   There are five types of ostrich – North African, Masai, Arabian, Somali, and Southern.

Owls

1959.   Owls are the only birds that can see the color blue.

1960.   There are 220 species of owl.

1961.   Owls have zygodactyl feet. This means they have two toes pointing forward and two pointing backward.

1962.   Although owls are associated with wisdom, they are the world's dumbest birds.

1963.   No single owl says "t'wit t'woo." A female brown owl says "t'wit" and the male responds by saying "t'woo."

1964.   Most owls have asymmetrical ears.

1965.   Most owls are silent when they fly.

1966.   Females are bigger and stronger than males.

1967.   Not all owls hoot. Most of them screech, whistle, bark, growl, rattle, or hiss.

1968.   Owls can be heard from a mile away.

1969.   Although owls are known for being nocturnal, some are only active during the day.

1970.   Although owls don't migrate, they can travel great distances when food is lacking.

1971.   A group of owls is called a parliament, a wisdom, a bazaar, or a study.

1972.   Baby owls are called owlets.

1973.   Owls eat insects, fish, rodents, and other owls.

1974.   Although their eyesight is exceptional, they can't really see objects too close to them.

1975.   The eyes of an owl are fixed in its sockets. To help see predators, it can turn its head 135 degrees.

1976.   A Barn Owl can eat up to 1,000 mice a year.

1977.   Owls can swallow mice whole.

Oysters

1978.   Oysters are filled with zinc. Eating them can help boost one's immune system, fight acne, and ease rashes.

1979.   There are only five kinds of oysters – Pacific, Kumamoto, European Flat, Atlantic, and Olympia. These can be separated into many subspecies.

1980.   Each oyster filters about 40 gallons of water a day.

1981.   Only certain types of oysters make pearls.

1982.   Pearls are the only gemstones made by living animals.

1983.   Removing a pearl will not kill the oyster.

1984.   Oysters can change their gender back and forth throughout their life.

1985.   Removing an oyster from its shell is called shucking.

1986.   The phrase, "The world is your oyster" comes from William Shakespeare's play, The Merry Wives of Windsor. The original quote was, "The world's mine oyster. Which I with sword will open."

1987.   Two billion pounds of oysters are eaten every year.

1988.   Originally, the chances of a pearl naturally growing in an oyster was 0.01%. However, humans have learned how to manipulate oysters so they will nearly always create a pearl.

1989.   Black pearls are the rarest and most desirable pearls in the world.

1990.   Pearl farming is known as periculture.

1991.   No two pearls are alike.

1992.   August 5th is National Oyster Day.

1993.   When a pearl is removed from an oyster, a little hole appears. This is called the "pearl's belly button."

1994.   Some Caribbean oysters can climb trees.

Pandas

1995.   When pandas are transported on a plane, they cannot be caged. They must be fastened with a seatbelt, wear a diaper, and sit beside their feeder.

Reminder – It is illegal to bring toothpaste onto a plane.

But a panda? Totally fine.

1996.   Only 1,000 pandas live in the wild.

1997.   Pandas are extremely territorial and will become violent if anything comes near them.

1998.   Pandas lean up against a wall upside down to defecate.

1999.   Female pandas are fertile for three days a year.

2000.   In Ancient times, the Chinese were scared of pandas, assuming they were as ferocious as a Grizzly Bear.

2001.   A panda has one of the strongest bites in the animal kingdom. They can tear apart a bamboo stalk with ease with their monstrous jaws. Humans, on the other hand, have difficulty cutting bamboo with an axe.

2002.   A panda's throat has a special lining to protect it from bamboo splinters.

2003.   "Panda" means "bamboo-eating animal."

2004.   There is only one species of panda. Its biological name is Ailuropoda melanoleuca, which means "black-and-white cat foot."

2005.   Pandas have to eat 80lbs of bamboo a day to meet their nutritional needs.

2006.   Richard Nixon owned two pandas.

2007.   Pandas live in Sichuan, Gansu, and Shaaxi in China.

2008.   Pandas don't hibernate.

2009.   Pandas mainly eat bamboo. A panda can eat an entire bamboo shoot in 40 seconds and eat 100lbs of bamboo daily.

2010.   Pandas walk with their front paws turned inward.

2011.   A panda's territory is about three square miles.

2012.   The WWF (World Wide Fund for Nature) has a panda as its logo because it saves money on printing.

2013.   Pandas relieve themselves about 40 times a day. They can excrete 62lbs worth of droppings per day.

2014.   Because pandas are so endangered, WWF are desperate to protect them in zoos. However, keeping a panda in a zoo is five times more expensive than keeping an elephant in a zoo.

2015.   Red pandas are raccoons, not pandas.

2016.   There is no recorded art of pandas until the 20th century.

2017.   Pandas have existed for three million years.

2018.   Panda fur is worth up to $100,000.

2019.   When baby pandas are born anywhere in the world, they are shipped by Fedex to China in order to expand the gene pool.

2020.   55% of a panda's life revolves around collecting, preparing, and eating bamboo.

2021.   Pandas live for 20 years.

2022.   For several years, researchers believed pandas were raccoons, not bears.

2023.   The Western world didn't know pandas existed until 1869.

2024.   An adult panda weighs 350lbs.

2025.   Chinese philosophers believed in Yin and Yang, which represents good and evil. The panda represents this due to its black-and-white colors and is seen as a sacred animal in China.

2026.   The eyespots of a panda cub are in the shape of a circle. As they grow older, they become tear-shaped.

2027.   They can stand upright but aren't able to walk this way.

2028.   A panda's skeleton is twice as heavy as any other animal of its size.

2029.   When a cub is born, it's pink.

2030.   Despite their vast size, newborn pandas only weigh 5oz when they are born. It takes two months before they reach the size of a newborn human baby.

2031. Pandas have extremely good visual memories and rely on it more than their spatial memory.

2032. They have 11 different calls.

2033. Pandas live alone because they don't have the energy to compete against other pandas.

2034. Its only predator is the snow leopard.

2035. Although their fur looks soft, its texture is surprisingly wiry.

2036. If the panda is wiped out, it will be the first time in modern history where an animal has gone extinct naturally rather than from human intervention.

2037. A panda's fur is black-and-white. Underneath the black fur is black skin. Underneath the white fur is pink skin.

2038. There are only 15 pandas in zoos outside of China.

2039. Chinese zoos contain 90 pandas.

2040. They roll down hills to remove twigs from their bodies.

2041. Pandas are the only bears that don't use facial expressions to communicate.

2042. Pandas can smell bamboo for miles.

2043. Pandas look like they have a thumb. In actual

fact, it is a modified wrist bone designed to hold bamboo.

2044.   You can be sentenced to death for killing a panda in China.

2045.   Pandas don't just eat bamboo. They also eat small rodents.

Parrots

2046.   There are 353 species of parrots.

2047.   Echo the parrot was placed in Witness Protection Program after testifying against his owner, which lead to his arrest.

2048.   There are two families of parrots – the Cacatuidae (cockatoos) and the Psittacidae (true parrots.)

2049.   If you ask a normal person what a parrot is, he or she will most certainly say it is "that bird that talks." However, only some parrots talk. A parrot is a bird with zygodactylous feet. This means that parrots have their first and fourth toes pointing backwards whereas their second and third toes point forward.

2050.   Parrots are one of the most intelligent birds in the world.

2051.   The most popular pet parrot is the budgerigar.

2052.   The Hyacinth Macaw is the largest parrot standing 1.3ft tall.

2053.   Parrots usually live for 80 years. The oldest one in recorded history lived for 87 years.

2054.   All parrots lay white eggs.

2055.   There are 11 million pet parrots in the US.

2056.   They usually sleep standing on one leg.

2057.   The African Grey can mimic voices better than any other parrot.

2058. No one truly knows why parrots can mimic sounds.

2059. President Andrew Jackson had a pet parrot. He got kicked out of Jackson's funeral for swearing.

Peafowls

2060.   A male peafowl is called a peacock. Its colorful fan-tail tail is its most identifiable feature.

2061.   The female peafowl is called a peahen. They do not have a fan-tail.

2062.   A peacock's tail is not used to woo females. Instead, it's used to intimidate predators. The tail looks like it has dozens of eyes, which frightens away larger animals.

2063.   There are three kinds of peafowls – Indian, green, and Congo.

2064.   The peacock's tail is called a train.

2065.   Peacocks fly into trees to hide from predators.

2066.   A group of peafowls is called a harem.

2067.   A baby peafowl is called a peachick.

2068.   It is a part of the pheasant family.

2069.   Peacocks live in India, Pakistan, and Sri Lanka.

2070.   They eat berries, figs, leaves, seeds, insects, and reptiles.

2071.   Their predators are tigers, leopards, and mongooses.

2072.   A peachick can walk, eat, and drink without assistance when it is one-day old.

2073.   Peahens live for 20 years.

2074.   In Greek myth, Zeus' wife, Hera, was usually depicted as a peacock.

<u>Pelicans</u>

2075.   A pelican can hold up to 2.5 gallons of water at a time in its gigantic beak.

2076.   A pelican's beak can shrink.

2077.   There are eight kinds of pelican.

2078.   They eat fish, tadpoles, crustaceans, and turtles.

2079.   They like to hunt in groups.

2080.   Although most pelicans are 4ft tall, some stand 6ft tall.

2081.   Pelicans have existed for 40 million years.

2082.   The Australian Pelican has the longest bird bill in the world, measuring 2ft.

2083.   The Dalmatian Pelican is the largest of its kind. Its wingspan can reach over 11ft wide.

2084.   A gull sometimes sits on pelican's head so it can steal the pelican's fish when the it opens its bill to pour out water.

2085.   Pelicans live for 30 years.

2086.   Despite the fact the pelican is one of the heaviest flying birds, its skeleton only makes up 10% of its weight.

Penguins

2087.   Zoologists can't decide how many species of penguin there are. Some say there are 17 species while others say there are 20.

2088.   The Emperor Penguin can dive up to 565 meters, which is deeper than any other bird. It is also deeper than the operational range of most naval submarines.

2089.   Baby penguins are called squabs.

2090.   The Emperor Penguin is the only bird that lays its eggs in the middle of winter. It does this so the squab can get through spring and summer after its born.

2091.   The Emperor Penguin can stay underwater for 27 minutes.

2092.   The Gentoo Penguin can swim 22mph, which is faster than any other bird.

2093.   The gender roles are reversed for the Emperor Penguin. The male incubates the egg while the female goes out to feed.

2094.   Penguins slide on their tummies over ice and snow. This is called tobogganing.

2095.   They eat fish, shrimp, krill, and crabs.

2096.   Penguins can eat 30 fish in one dive.

2097.   It is the only animal that has a diet consisting purely of fish and crustaceans. This makes the penguin a piscivorous creature.

2098. Penguins have seconds to transfer their eggs to each other or the egg will freeze and the fetus inside will die.

2099. If a mother penguin loses her squab, she sometimes tries to steal an egg from another family.

2100. Penguins are able to control their blood flow.

2101. A group of penguins is called a rookery. This is also the name of their nest.

2102. The Galapagos penguin is the only penguin that lives in the tropics.

2103. It is illegal to eat penguins in the US.

2104. Most penguins swim at 4-7mph.

2105. Penguins spend more of their life in the ocean than on land.

2106. Penguins replace their feathers every year.

2107. The Emperor Penguin is the largest penguin. It's 3.7ft and weighs 77lbs.

2108. Penguins have knees.

2109. There are no penguins in the Arctic.

2110. Penguins only lay two eggs per year.

2111. Millions of years ago, penguins were nearly 7ft tall.

2112. They spend hours preening their feathers every

day.

2113.   Their feathers molt every year. They can't go into
water until their feathers regrow.

2114.   The most common penguin is the Macaroni
Penguin. There are approximately 23 million
worldwide.

2115.   Penguins recognize one another from their calls
rather than from their appearance.

2116.   During the winter, penguins can lose 33% of
their body weight.

2117.   Astonishingly, a penguin's body temperature is
only 38 degrees Celsius. That's only one degree higher
than a human's body temperature.

2118.   Emperor Penguins have the longest
uninterrupted incubation of any bird at 67 days.

2119.   Morgan Freeman narrated the 2005
documentary, March of the Penguins, in one day.

2120.   When March of the Penguins was released, it was
the second highest grossing theatrical documentary
ever.

2121.   Emperor Penguins have the widest variety of
vocalizations of all penguins.

2122.   King Penguins can form nesting colonies of
10,000 penguins.

2123.   Gentoo Penguins are the only penguins that have
long tails.

2124.   Little Penguins are the smallest of their kind, measuring 16 inches high and weighing 2lbs.

2125.   Although penguins have great vision underwater, they are near-sighted on land.

2126.   King Penguins sing songs to their partners.

2127.   Penguins evolved from the Waimanu manneringi. This creature existed 60 million years ago.

2128.   Penguins can drink salt water because they have a special gland that filters salt from the bloodstream.

2129.   0.002% of penguins are born with brown plumage instead of black plumage. They are called isabelline penguins. They don't live very long because they can't camouflage themselves.

2130.   Penguins live in South Africa, New Zealand, Chile, Argentina, Antarctica, and Australia.

2131.   Oscar-nominated actor, Benedict Cumberbatch, narrated a documentary about penguins and starred in the film, Penguins of Madagascar, in spite of the fact that he can't pronounce the word "penguins" correctly. Instead, he says "penguings."

2132.   A group of squabs is called a crèche.

2133.   A group of penguins in water is called a raft.

2134.   Penguins aren't afraid of humans.

2135.   The Emperor Penguins is the most feathered birds in the world, having 100 feathers per square inch.

2136.   The Chinstrap Penguins are nicknamed "Stonecrackers" because their cry is so loud, biologists joked that it could split a stone in half.

2137.   Millions of years ago, penguins could fly.

2138.   They are the most aquatic birds in the world.

2139.   The rarest penguin is the Yellow-Eyed Penguin. Only 5,000 exist worldwide.

2140.   Penguins enter and leave the sea in large numbers to minimize being attacked by a predator.

2141.   Penguins can't taste fish.

<u>Pigs</u>

2142.   Although "sweating like a pig" is a popular phrase, pigs can't really sweat because they have very few sweat glands.

2143.   Pigs cover themselves in mud to minimize exposure to the Sun or they will dehydrate.

2144.   Newborn piglets will leave their nest to urinate within hours of birth.

2145.   Pigs have to arrange their sleeping den every night. They are extremely particular and will start over if it is not satisfactory.

2146.   Pigs mate up to 30 times a day.

2147.   Big Major Cay is an island in the Bahamas populated by pigs. No humans live on the island.

2148.   Pigs were domesticated 7,000 years ago.

2149.   There are two billion pigs worldwide.

2150.   48 pigs were used to play the title character in the film, Babe.

2151.   Female pigs usually give birth to a litter of 12 pigs. The most pigs ever born in a single litter was 37.

2152.   Pigs are one of the smartest animals in the world.

2153.   Pigs are susceptible to sunburn.

2154.   Miss Piggy from The Muppets was originally called Piggy Lee.

2155. Pigs are excellent swimmers.

2156. There are feral pigs in all but three states in the US.

2157. There are more feral pigs in Denmark than people.

2158. Pigs understand how mirrors work.

2159. Although pigs have four toes on each foot, they tip-toe on two toes.

2160. March 1st is National Pig Day in the US.

2161. Pigs used to be kept on ships because the crew believed that if there was a shipwreck, the pig would always swim to the nearest shore.

2162. Pigs live for 15 years.

2163. Some hogs have tusks. However, the babirusa is a pig that looks like it has tusks when it actually has teeth growing from its jaws out of its mouth. Because these teeth never stop growing, the babirusa needs to file them down or the pig will impale its own skull, killing itself.

2164. Pigs can drink 14 gallons a day.

2165. Winston Churchill once said, "Dogs look up to man. Cats look down to man. Pigs look us straight in the eye and see an equal."

2166. In Ancient Egypt, pigs were seen as a symbol of fertility.

2167. Feral pigs cause $1.5 billion worth of agricultural

damage every year.

2168.   They have a heightened sense of smell and can find things underground based on its scent.

2169.   Some tattooists practice tattoos on pigs before they perform the procedure on humans.

2170.   A pig's heart is so similar to a human's, it's very common for a pig's valve to replace a human one when a person's heart is impaired.

2171.   You know what's weirder than putting pig organs into humans? Growing human organs in pigs. On June 6th 2016, scientists at the University of California have begun plans to create a pig-human chimera.
        Experiments like this have been done on other animals but never survived beyond the fetus. If this experiment is successful, a shortage of organ transplants could be a thing of the past.

2172.   A group of pigs is called a herd. However, a group of 12 pigs or more is called a sounder.

2173.   Half of the pigs in the world are in China.

2174.   Pigs are very peaceful. Sows will only show aggression when their piglets are threatened.

2175.   The pig is the last of the 12 animals in the Chinese zodiac. In China, the pig is a symbol of happiness, fortune, and honesty.

2176.   Pigs make over 20 different noises.

2177.   Micro pigs (also known as mini pigs or teacup pigs) have been bred recently and have become a popular pet. And yes, they are so small, they can fit in a teacup. However, zoologists state that breeding small pigs is incredibly unhealthy. They are also one of the most common pets to be abandoned since they suffer many organ problems.

2178.   The largest pig ever was Big Bill. He weighed a gargantuan 2,552lbs. He was 5ft tall and 9ft long. He was so big, his stomach dragged on the ground.

Pigeons

2179.   The Chinese army have pigeons ready as a backup form of communication in case their electronic systems gets shut down.

2180.   Charles Darwin said that observing pigeons convinced him that evolution was a real concept.

2181.   Pigeons were domesticated 6,000 years ago.

2182.   Although sources say pigeons are infested with disease, there is no information to back this up.

2183.   A pigeon can accelerate from standing still to 60mph in two seconds. This means that a pigeon has better acceleration than a Ferrari.

2184.   Before 1840, there were millions of passenger pigeons. They went extinct in 1914.

2185.   There's 350 types of pigeon.

2186.   Pigeons can be taught to distinguish every letter of the alphabet.

2187.   Pigeons live for 30 years.

2188.   Pigeons mate for life.

2189.   Female pigeons can give birth when they are seven months old.

2190.   10 days after mating, the female lays 1-3 eggs, which hatch after 18 days.

2191.   Pigeons are the most common urban bird in the

world.

2192. The pigeon is the only bird that don't have to lift its head to swallow.

2193. Homing pigeons fly up to 700 miles a day.

2194. There are 400 million pigeons worldwide.

2195. Pigeons can hear sounds that are 11 octaves below middle C, which allows them to detect earthquakes and electrical storms.

2196. Pigeons are still used today by the Swiss, French, Israelis, and the Iraqis to transfer important information.

2197. The first known pigeon was the Middle Eastern Rock pigeon.

2198. A pigeon has 10,000 feathers.

2199. Pigeons can fly 77.6mph. The fastest pigeon ever flew 92.5mph.

2200. Pigeons don't leave the nest until they are mature. This is why you never see pigeon chicks.

2201. Pigeons can fly as high as 6,000ft.

2202. Pigeons can move their wings 10 times per second.

2203. Their heart beats 600 times per minute.

2204. Pigeons have no depth perception. As a result, they constantly bob their heads to gauge how far away objects are.

Platypuses

2205.   When the duck-billed platypus was discovered, scientists didn't think it was a real animal. They assumed that somebody was playing a joke on them and the animal was a beaver with a duck-bill glued to its face.

2206.   Platypuses swim with their eyes closed.

2207.   Platypuses are venomous. Although their venom won't kill a human, it is extremely painful.

2208.   They live in Australia and Tasmania.

2209.   It is a part of the Ornithorhynchidae family. All of its relatives have gone extinct.

2210.   Platypuses eat worms, larvae, and shrimp.

2211.   The platypus detects its prey by picking up electromagnetic waves by placing its bill underwater.

2212.   They walk on their knuckles.

2213.   The only mammals that lay eggs are platypuses and pangolins.

<u>Polar Bears</u>

2214.   If you ate a polar bear liver, you would overdose on vitamin A.

2215.   Polar bears have black skin.

2216.   Polar bears don't have white fur. Their fur is reflective and it absorbs light, which makes it look white.

2217.   In the 1st century, polar bears fought seals in Roman amphitheaters.

2218.   A polar bear can swim 60 miles without stopping.

2219.   Less than 2% of polar bears' hunts are successful.

2220.   When a polar bear is born, it's the size of a guinea pig.

2221.   Polar bears clean themselves by rolling in snow.

2222.   Polar bears live in the Arctic where the temperature can drop to -50 degrees Celsius. In spite of this, polar bears have a serious problem with overheating! Since they have naturally adapted to intense cold, they struggle during the summer when the temperature is above freezing.

2223.   A group of polar bears is called a celebration or an aurora.

2224.   Polar bears are the largest land predators. They stand 11ft high and weigh over 1,700lbs.

2225.   Polar bears originally came from Ireland.

Rabbits

2226.   Rabbits and parrots are the only animals that can see behind themselves without turning their head.

2227.   A group of rabbits is called a nest.

2228.   The world's largest rabbit is called Darius. He stands 4.3ft and weighs 50lbs. He's insured for $1.6 million.

2229.   Rabbits can run up to 40mph.

2230.   Baby rabbits are born furless.

2231.   Females can produce eight litters of rabbits per year.

2232.   A baby rabbit is called a kit.

2233.   Rabbits don't open their eyes until they are two weeks old.

2234.   There is a superstition that possessing a rabbit's foot will bring good luck. However, the original superstition was that the rabbit's foot would become lucky if the rabbit died in a graveyard. The eviler the person buried there, the luckier the token will supposedly be. President Grover Cleveland allegedly carried a rabbit foot that he found on the grave of Western outlaw, Jesse James.

2235.   The largest rabbit litter ever consisted of 24 kits.

2236.   Rabbits live for about seven years. The oldest rabbit ever was 16 years old.

2237. A rabbit's heart can beat up to 325 times per minute.

2238. About two million US households have a pet rabbit.

2239. Their teeth never stop growing.

2240. They can jump 3ft vertically.

2241. A group of baby rabbits is called wrack.

Raccoons

2242.   Raccoons do not hibernate.

2243.   They can climb trees with ease and can fall 40ft without hurting themselves.

2244.   Raccoons tend to live 16 years in the wild or 21 years in captivity.

2245.   Although they rarely approach water, raccoons are excellent swimmers.

2246.   They have one litter per year. Each litter is made up of 3-7 babies.

2247.   They eat grapes, cherries, nuts, acorns, berries, apples, plums, peaches, insects, frogs, fish, crayfish, and bird eggs.

2248.   They are nocturnal.

2249.   Raccoons can make over 200 different sounds.

2250.   They are preyed on by hawks, owls, and wolves.

2251.   A group of raccoons is called a gaze.

2252.   Raccoons are covered in parasites. The worst one is the raccoon roundworm, which can cause blindness and even death in humans.

Rats

2253.   The reason why rat poison is so effective is because rats can't vomit.

2254.   Rats don't have good eyesight so they rely on their whiskers to know what's around them.

2255.   Although rats are always seen as being filthy and disgusting, they clean themselves more often that cats.

2256.   Rats like chocolate.

2257.   They recognise their name and can be taught to do tricks.

2258.   If you are thinking of buying one as a pet, it's better to buy a pair as they get lonely when they are by themselves.

2259.   Rats love swimming.

2260.   They sleep 75% of the time.

2261.   Their long tail gives them a great sense of balance, which makes them amazing climbers.

2262.   Rats can get their intertwined, forcing them to live as one. A group of interlocked rats is called a Rat King and can consists of up to 30 rats.

Reptiles

2263. A reptile is a cold-blooded scaly vertebrate that lays eggs. However, there are exceptions to this rule. For example, the skink produces live young but is classified as a reptile.

2264. Reptiles have a four-chambered heart.

2265. There are 8,240 species of reptiles in the world.

2266. The term "cold-blooded" is often associated with reptiles. However, it's misleading because reptiles don't actually have cold blood. The term refers to the fact that the reptile can't heat itself like the mammals do. Reptiles rely on external sources to stay warm.

2267. Based on their appearance, it's easy to assume reptiles have a slimy exterior. However, because they lack sweat glands, their skin usually feels cool and dry.

2268. Many reptiles (especially snakes) have scales made of keratin. Keratin is a protein that can be found in human hair and fingernails.

2269. Lizards and snakes have a single sheet of overlapping scales. Some reptiles grow plates (separate areas of scales.) The main function of a reptile's plates is to keep water in the animal's body. This is how reptiles can go a long time without water.

2270. Many reptiles thrive in deserts.

2271. Reptiles can control their pupil size.

2272. The fastest reptile is the Spiny-Tailed Iguana. It can run 21.7mph.

2273.   A reptile's brain usually makes up 1% of its body size.

2274.   The oldest known reptile is the Hylonomus Lyelli. This lizard was eight inches long and lived 320 million years ago.

2275.   Modern scientists classify birds as a subspecies of reptiles. Birds evolved from reptiles millions of years ago.

Rhinoceroses

2276.   The word "rhinoceros" means "nose horn."

2277.   Black Rhinos and White Rhinos are both grey.

2278.   Rhinos don't have horns since a horn must have bone cartilage. Although most sources say a rhino's "horn" is made of hair, biologists classify it as a nail. Poachers kill rhinos for their "horn" to cure fevers. However, the "horn" has proven to have no effect on a person's well-being.
    There are some sources that say the horn is used as an aphrodisiac. This isn't true.

2279.   A group of rhinos is called a crash.

2280.   There are five kinds of rhino – the Black Rhino, the White Rhino, the Indian Rhino, the Javan Rhino, and the Sumatran Rhino. There are also 11 subspecies of rhino.

2281.   Sumatran rhinos have two "horns."

2282.   In 1900, there were 500,000 rhinos worldwide. Now, there are 29,000.

2283.   When they get too hot, rhinos soak themselves in mud.

2284.   Rhinos usually weigh 3,000lbs.

2285.   The White Rhino is the largest type. It is 6ft tall, 13ft long and weighs up to 7,700lbs.

2286.   Three of the five rhino species are critically endangered. There are less than 100 Sumatran rhinos and there are only 35 Javan rhinos worldwide.

2287.   Baby rhinos are called calves.

2288.   A rhino calf weighs 140lbs when it's born.

2289.   Rhinos live for 45 years.

2290.   A rhino calf will set out on its own when it turns three years old.

2291.   Females are pregnant for 16 months.

2292.   Despite the fact that rhinos look like a living tank, their skin is sensitive to sunburn and insect bites.

2293.   Some rhinos use their teeth to defend themselves instead of their "horn."

2294.   Although they don't hang out with other rhinos, they don't mind the company of birds. This is because certain birds like oxpeckers eat mites and other insects on the rhino's hide. Also, birds panic when they sense danger, which gives the rhino a warning.

2295.   Rhinos have terrible eyesight but have a great sense of smell and hearing.

2296.   A female gives birth every 3-5 years. They usually give birth to a single calf but occasionally have twins.

2297.   Rhinos have existed for 50 million years.

2298.   They can run up to 40 mph.

2299.   Black Rhinos fight each and have the highest death rate among mammals of the same species.

2300. Rhinos are genetically related to horses, tapirs, zebras, and donkeys.

Scorpions

2301.   Sometimes, pseudoscorpions grab hold of flies'
legs to transport itself to a new location.

2302.   Of the 1,500 species of scorpions, 95% of them
are harmless to humans. Only 23 people are killed by
scorpions every year.

2303.   The most venomous scorpions are the
Deathstalker, the Arizona Bark Scorpion, the Fattail
Scorpion, and the Emperor Scorpion.

2304.   Most scorpions are only 0.5 inches long.

2305.   The largest scorpion measure 7.5 inches.

2306.   Scorpions have been around for 430 million
years.

2307.   Scorpions can live for up to 10 years.

2308.   Baby scorpions are called scorplings.

2309.   Scorplings ride on their mother's back for the
first few weeks of life.

2310.   Most scorpions have six eyes. Some scorpion
species have 12 eyes. Despite this, they have terrible
vision and rely on picking up vibrations.

2311.   The correct term for its tail is the metasoma.

2312.   The correct term for its head is the prosoma.

2313.   Some scorpions can live without food or water
for over a year.

2314.   They are nocturnal and will usually hide in holes or under rocks during the day.

2315.   Scorpions are fluorescent under ultraviolet light. Scientists don't know why.

2316.   A sea scorpion called the Jaekelopteus lived 390 million years ago. It was the largest scorpion ever, measuring 8.1ft.

2317.   If a scorpion absorbs alcohol, it will go berserk and sting itself to death.

Seahorses

2318.   Seahorses are the only fish that swim upright.

2319.   They use pectoral fins behind their eyes to steer.

2320.   Seahorses are the only fish that have a neck.

2321.   When resting, they usually wrap their tail around a stationary object.

2322.   They can move each eye independently.

2323.   They eat fish, plankton, and shrimp.

2324.   Seahorses have existed for over three million years.

2325.   Although many sources state that seahorses are monogamous, this is false.

2326.   They are nicknamed "the stallions of the sea."

2327.   Seahorses are the slowest fish. An average seahorse moves 0.01mph.

2328.   At birth, as many as 1,500 baby seahorses can be born at once. However, seahorses don't nurture their young in any way. Unsurprisingly, less than 1% of seahorses reach adulthood.

2329.   Seahorses can change into a variety of colors in seconds.

2330.   Most seahorses are 3cm long.

2331.   There are 53 species of seahorses.

2332. They don't have teeth or stomachs.

2333. A seahorse can eat 4,000 brine shrimp per day.

2334. After the seahorse becomes pregnant, she transfers the egg to the male's pouch, where it will fertilize until it's ready to emerge.

Seals

2335.   Seals, sea lions, and walruses are pinnipeds, which means "fin-footed" in Latin.

2336.   Seals have furry, stubby front feet. Their thinly webbed flippers have a claw on each small toe.

2337.   It's easy to mix up a seal and a sea lion. However, if you look at the two animals beside each other, you can see that they look dramatically different. A sea lion can walk on land with its flippers but a seal can't.
      Sea lions are noisy while seals are quiet and vocalize via soft grunts.
      Sea lions have small flaps for outer ears while true seas (also known as earless seals) lack external ears.
      Seals are far more adapted to the sea than sea lions.

2338.   A group of seals is called a raft and contain up to 1,500 seals.

2339.   The Baikal seal is the only seal found exclusively in fresh water.

2340.   There are 18 species of true seals according to Seals World.

2341.   The largest seal is the Southern Elephant Seal. It can measure 20ft long and weigh 8,500lbs. That's dramatically heavier than a walrus.

2342.   True seals can be found in the Arctic or off the coasts of Antarctica.

2343.   Seals eat octopus, lobster, squid, fish, and eel. Some of them eat penguins.

2344.   Seal milk is 50% fat.

2345.   It can hold its breath for two hours, which is longer than any other mammal.

2346.   They can dive up to 1,300ft deep.

2347.   Their predators are orca, Polar Bears, and sharks.

2348.   Seals will bite humans if they get too close.

2349.   They live for 46 years.

2350.   Seals give birth on land.

Sharks

2351.   Great White Sharks have 300 serated teeth that are separated into seven rows.

2352.   A Great White is 15ft long and weighs 5,000lbs.

2353.   Humans have killed over 2.8 million Great Whites during the 20th century.

2354.   Great Whites can go months without eating.

2355.   A Great White can see 10 times better at night than a human can during the day.

2356.   Whale Sharks are the world's largest fish. They can grow up to 50ft and weigh 40,000 lbs.

2357.   Whale Sharks have no teeth and are harmless to humans.

2358.   The Whale Shark lays the largest egg in the world. The egg measures 2ft long.

2359.   A baby shark is called a pup.

2360.   Statistically, you are more likely to be killed by a sandcastle than a shark.

2361.   Shark corneas have been used in human eye transplants.

2362.   Whale Sharks produce more pups than any other shark. They can give birth to over 100 pups at a time.

2363.   The Goblin Shark has only been seen 50 times in the last century.

2364. Female sharks instinctively lose their appetite when they give birth so they won't be tempted to eat their pups.

2365. There are sources that say that sharks have stopped evolving, they can't stop moving, and they can't get cancer. None of these statements are true.

2366. Rays and skates have evolved from sharks.

2367. Sharks have no bones. Their skeleton is made of cartilage.

2368. There's a shark called the Ninja Lanternshark.
Now, you might think an eight-year-old came up with that name.
Actually, it was two eight-year-olds. If the name sounds silly, it was nearly called the Super Ninja Shark.
Its name is justified since its organs can glow in the dark like a lantern, meaning it can appear and disappear in an instant like a ninja.

2369. Killer Whales kill Great White Sharks. When a Killer Whale shredded a Great White near California's Farallon Islands in 2000, the blood of the shark terrified every other shark and made them all swim away. One Great White was tagged with a chip and could be seen to instantly dive to a depth of 500 metres. When he thought he was safe, he then swam...to Hawaii.

2370. When a shark is about to attack, it hunches its back, lowers its pectoral fins, and swims in a zigzag motion.

2371. The Shortfin Mako Shark can accelerate faster than a Porsche.

2372.   Shark teeth are covered in fluoride, which works like toothpaste. This keeps the shark's mouth healthy and clean.

2373.   Some sharks are pregnant for up to four years.

2374.   Humans kill 11,417 sharks every hour.

2375.   Probably the strangest shark to ever exist was the Helicoprion. It had a circular saw for teeth.

2376.   Female sharks have much thicker skin than male sharks.

2377.   50 species of shark glow in the dark.

2378.   The Cigar Shark is so-called because it is shaped like a cigar. However, since it creates perfect circles when it bites down on its prey, it is also known as the Cookiecutter Shark.

2379.   Herodotus (who lived from 484-425B.C.) was the first person to write an account of a shark attack. He described a horde of "monsters" that had devoured shipwrecked sailors of the Persian fleet.

2380.   If a shark eats something it can't digest like a turtle's shell, it can thrust its own stomach out of its mouth to vomit out the undigested item before pulling its stomach back in.

2381.   Sharks can grow a new set of teeth in eight days.

2382.   The prehistoric Megaladon Shark was twice the size of a Tyrannosaurus Rex. It was so big that it could effortlessly fit an entire Great White into its mouth.

2383.   If a shark flips over, it will go into a coma.

2384.   The Greenland Shark eats Polar Bears.

2385.   The Greenland Shark lives for up to 200 years.

2386.   Thousands of cables lie in the ocean which allow Internet access worldwide. However, engineers have to keep fixing the cables because sharks keep nibbling them.

2387.   As soon as Tiger Shark embryos develop teeth, they attack and eat each other while in the womb.

2388.   Sharks can instinctively increase their body temperature.

2389.   Sharks are the only fish that have eyelids.

2390.   Sharks know exactly where their prey is even if it is a mile away and is isn't moving.

2391.   A shark's jaw isn't attached to its cranium.

2392.   Sharkskin was used millennia ago to polish wood.

2393.   Sharks were originally known as "sea dogs."

2394.   Sharks kill about five people per year.

2395.   The word "shark" comes from the German word, "Schorck," which is a variant of "shurke," which means "scoundrel villain."

2396.   Sharks are far more likely to attack men than

women. Nobody knows why.

2397.   Only 30 species of shark are dangerous to humans.

2398.   Sharks can swim in very shallow water. A 9ft long Bull Shark can swim in water even if it is 2ft deep. In fact, 66% of shark attacks have occurred in water that was only 6ft deep and most shark attacks occur less than 100ft from the shore.

2399.   The most common shark attacks occur in Florida, Hawaii, Australia, and South Africa.

2400.   A shark's liver makes up 25% of its total weight.

2401.   Bull Sharks can live in salt water and fresh water.

2402.   The Tiger Shark usually preys on birds before they have learned how to fly.

2403.   Sharks are so efficient at conserving energy when they swim, inventors have used their techniques to improve yachts and submarines.

2404.   The largest Great White ever found was 17ft long and weighed 2,664lbs.

2405.   In the film, Jaws IV: The Revenge, there is a scene where the shark roars... even though sharks don't have lungs.

2406.   The rarest shark is the Megamouth. Only 14 have ever been seen and the first was spotted in 1976. It earns its name due to its 3ft wide mouth.

2407.   All animals emit small electrical signals when

they breathe or move. However, most animals can't detect these signals. Sharks are considered to be the best animals on Earth at picking up on these electric signals.

2408.   Sharks usually attack metal objects because they give off electric signals.

2409.   Shoes made of shark leather will last four times longer than normal leather.

2410.   A Wobbegong Shark is so flat, that it looks like it's part of the sea floor.

2411.   Native Americans used shark teeth as arrow heads.

2412.   A shark's skin is made of denticles instead of scales.

2413.   The shark's greatest sense is its hearing. It can hear prey two miles away.

2414.   Nurse Sharks are the laziest shark. They crawl around the sea floor like vacuum cleaners sucking up any prey it can find.

2415.   The Dwarf Lantern Shark is the smallest shark. It's less than 0.6ft long.

2416.   Hammerhead Sharks are the newest form of sharks to exist. They are only 20 million years old, while most sharks have existed for 450 million years.

2417.   Sharks can smell one drop of blood from 100 million droplets of water and tell which direction it came from.

2418.   Sharks have small holes on their sides called lateral line organs, which are very sensitive to small movements near them. This is how a shark can tell if fish are in their proximity even if the shark can't see them.

2419.   Sharks don't like the taste of human flesh. After they have a bite, they usually swim away to find something else to eat.

2420.   The Great White is the only fish to poke its head above the water to observe its surroundings.

2421.   The Tiger Shark is nicknamed the "garbage can of the sea" because it will eat absolutely anything.

2422.   The Tiger Shark is the second-most dangerous shark.

2423.   Of the 400 types of shark, only 20% of them are larger than humans.

2424.   If you rubbed a shark's nose, it will become incredibly disorientated.

2425.   Peter Benchley is one of the greatest shark protectors in the world. Ironically, he is the writer of Jaws, which inspired the summer blockbuster of the same name.

Sheep

2426.   A group of sheep is called a flock, a fold, or a herd.

2427.   A baby sheep can be called a lamb, a lambkin, or a cosset.

2428.   Sheep can recognize up to 50 faces. They can recognize a human face for up to two years.

2429.   Sheep's wool has been used by humans for 12,000 years.

2430.   A sheep can produce up to 30lbs per wool a year.

2431.   In the US, 1lb of wool is worth about $1.15.

2432.   Sheep are about seven times larger now than they were during the Middle Ages.

2433.   Sheep and shepherds are mentioned in the Bible 247 times.

2434.   There are 145 million sheep in Australia, which produce 80% of the wool used in clothing. The industry is worth $2.8 billion per year.

2435.   A sheep's wool secretes an oily substance called lanolin. It is used to make chewing gum chewier.

2436.   The Ancient Egyptians used to mummify sheep.

2437.   There's over a billion sheep worldwide.

2438.   There are 900 different breeds of sheep.

2439.   The fleece of one sheep can be spun to produce a 124-mile-long strand.

2440.   Sheep weigh about 150lbs. Some can weigh up to 350lbs.

2441.   There are more sheep in China than any other country.

2442.   The ram, Aries, is the first sign of the Zodiac.

2443.   A male sheep is called a ram. A castrated male is called a wether. A female sheep is called a ewe.

2444.   Their eyes are so far apart, they have a field of vision of 300 degrees.

2445.   Sheep normally live for 5-10 years.

2446.   Ewes usually give birth to 1-3 lambs at a time.

2447.   Experts can tell the mood of a sheep by looking at the position of its ears.

2448.   Sheep can recognize when they're ill and will eat specific plants to heal themselves.

2449.   Sheep are gregarious, which means they like to be in a group.

2450.   Sheep are precocial, which means they are highly independent from birth.

Shrews

2451. Although rodents usually have incisor teeth that never stop growing, a shrew's teeth eventually wear down.

2452. A Masked Shrew's heart beats 1,200 times a minute. That's faster than any other animal on Earth.

2453. A shrew's metabolic rate is so high that it has to eat 90% of its body weight of food daily to survive. They will starve if they don't eat within 12 hours.

2454. Shrews are so easily startled, they can die of shock if they hear a loud noise.

2455. They eat worms, fish, frogs, seeds, and nuts.

2456. Shrews are nocturnal.

2457. They have poor vision and rely on their smell and hearing.

2458. They are very smart animals. Their brain makes up 10% of their body weight.

2459. Although shrews are killed by other mammals, they are rarely eaten because they have a gland that releases a disgusting stench when they die.

2460. Shrews live for about 1-2 years.

2461. Females have about 10 litters a year.

2462. The Etruscan Shrew is 3.5cm and weighs 2g, making it the smallest terrestrial mammal in the world.

2463.   Although they don't make tunnels, they hide in holes created by moles.

2464.   Some shrews are venomous.

2465.   Short-Tailed Shrews are so vicious, they can easily kill venomous scorpions.

<u>Shrimp</u>

2466.   Like other crustaceans, shrimps have 10 legs.

2467.   Shrimp swim backwards.

2468.   The Mantis Shrimp can swing its claws so fast, it boils the water around it.

2469.   The Mantis Shrimp can see four times more colors than a human.

2470.   Americans eat a billion shrimp per year.

2471.   There are 600 species of shrimp.

2472.   The Skeleton Shrimp has a transparent body and poisonous claws.

2473.   May 9th is National Shrimp Day.

2474.   April 29th is National Shrimp Scampi Day. I don't know why there are two days dedicated to shrimp and only one day dedicated to Martin Luther King.

2475.   They can lay up to a million eggs at a time.

2476.   An average shrimp lives for 18 months.

2477.   Over five billion pounds of shrimp is produced annually.

2478.   Shrimp are usually 0.5ft long.

2479.   The longest shrimp ever found was 1.4ft long.

2480.   There are 16 different stages of life of a shrimp

from egg to full adult.

2481.   Their predators are crabs, whales, sea urchins, and dolphins.

Skunks

2482. A human can smell a skunk's stench from a mile away.

2483. A skunk can spray and bite at the same time.

2484. A skunk does a handstand to warn predators that it is ready to spray.

2485. They can shoot their spray up to 10ft.

2486. The official name for the skunk family is Mephitidae, which means "stink."

2487. A skunk's spray is highly flammable.

2488. The most well-known breed is the Striped Skunk. However, there are other skunks such as the Eastern Spotted Skunk, the Hooded Skunk, and the Hog-Nosed Skunk.

2489. Skunks eat insects, wasps, worms, and grubs.

2490. Skunks are immune to snake venom.

2491. They have long nails, which makes them excellent diggers. They tend to dig holes in lawns and gardens.

2492. A group of skunks is called a surfeit.

Sloths

2493.   Sloths are long-armed mammals that live in trees in Central America and South America. They are known for being extremely slow and lazy. Many predators' eyesight is based on moving targets, which means that they usually don't spot sloths.

2494.   Although many sources state that sloths sleep for 20 hours a day, they only sleep for 10 hours.

2495.   They are incredible swimmers.

2496.   They urinate and defecate once a week. They have to defecate and urinate at the same time.

2497.   Some sloths look green because algae grows on their fur.

2498.   Their predators are eagles, snakes, and jaguars.

2499.   Three-toed sloths can turn their heads almost 360 degrees.

2500.   Sloths can hang onto branches even after they have died.

2501.   They are nocturnal.

2502.   Sloths are solitary and only gather to mate.

2503.   A hairless sloth was discovered in Panama City several years ago. A group of teenagers thought it was an alien and ran away.

2504.   Sloths live for 40 years.

2505. Giant Sloths went extinct about 3,500 years ago. They were 17ft tall. That's larger than an African Elephant.

2506. Sloths sometimes fall to their death because they mistake their own arm as a branch.

Slugs

2507. Slugs like beer.

2508. Slugs can switch gender to fertilize their own eggs.

2509. The Banana Slug is the largest slug, measuring almost 1ft long.

2510. Slugs live for 1-6 years.

2511. Although most slugs eat rotting vegetation, some of them are carnivorous.

2512. A slug has green blood.

2513. 95% of slugs live underground.

2514. Slugs lay 20-100 eggs per year.

2515. Slugs and snails are gastropods, which means "stomach foot."

2516. Slugs used to live in the sea.

2517. An acre of farmland has about 250,000 slugs.

2518. Slugs follow their own slime to find their way home.

2519. A slug's slime absorbs water, which is why it's so hard to wash off.

2520. A slug's slime has fibers, which prevents it from sliding down vertical surfaces.

2521. Since it has no bones, slugs can stretch 20 times its

normal length, which allows it to squeeze through tiny openings.

2522.   Vinegar is effective at getting rid of slug slime.

2523.   A slug has one lung.

2524.   Slug eggs can lay dormant for years and won't hatch until the conditions are right.

2525.   The idea that "snails have shells and slugs don't" isn't true. The difference between the two species is genetic and is only physically visible to experts.

Snails

2526.   A snail can pass over the edge of a razor blade without hurting itself.

2527.   The smallest snail is the Acmella nana, which measures 0.7mm.

2528.   A snail has 25,600 teeth. They are separated in hundreds of rows in its mouth.

2529.   A snail can regrow an eye if it loses one.

2530.   Some snails hibernate.

2531.   Snails can live for 25 years.

2532.   The Giant African Land Snail is the biggest snail, measuring 1ft long.

2533.   Garden snails have a top speed of 50 yards per hour. That's 1.3cm per second.

2534.   Snails can see but they can't hear.

2535.   A snail will die if salt is poured on it.

2536.   They can lift up to 10 times their own body weight.

2537.   Snails eat 500 different types of plants.

2538.   A group of snails is called an escargatoire.

Snakes

2539. The Titanboa is the biggest, longest, and heaviest snake ever. It was 48ft long and weighed 2,500 lbs.

2540. There are 3,400 types of snakes.

2541. Snake-charming snakes respond to movement, not sound.

2542. A single drop of Sea Snake venom can kill three people.

2543. A group of cobras is called a quiver.

2544. Snakes don't have eyelids. They have to sleep with their eyes open.

2545. Snakes can tell when other animals are nearby by detecting vibrations in the ground.

2546. The smallest snake is the 10cm Thread Snake.

2547. A group of snakes is called a ball or a rhumba.

2548. The snake that causes the most human deaths is the Saw-Scaled Viper. It lives in West Africa.

2549. The longest snake is the 22.8-ft-long Reticulated Python.

2550. If you got bitten by a Boomslang Snake, you would bleed from every orifice in your body.

2551. Despite what many sources say, snakes do not dislocate their mouth when they open it. However, they can open their mouth up to 150 degrees.

2552. A bite from a Black Mamba is almost always lethal.

2553. Black Mambas are grey or brown but never black.

2554. Although it only takes one bite from a Black Mamba to kill a human, they can strike 12 times in a row.

2555. If a snake's meal is too big, its stomach can explode.

2556. Snakes can have up to 200 teeth.

2557. In 2014, Paul Rosolie attempted to be the first person to survive being swallowed by an anaconda. He gave up once the snake started breaking his arm.

2558. Some snakes can survive without eating for two years.

2559. Snake teeth point backwards to prevent their swallowed prey from escaping its throat.

2560. A constrictor is a snake that wraps itself around its prey and crushes it to death. Pythons are the only constrictors that have caused human deaths.

2561. The Death Adder has the fastest strike of any snake in the world. It can attack, inject its venom, and return to its original position in under 0.15 seconds.

2562. Many venomous snakes will explode if they digest Alka-Seltzer.

2563. A python can swallow a whole alligator.

2564.   If a Tiger Snake bites you, you have a 50% chance of survival. However, it is illegal to kill these snakes because they are endangered.

2565.   Anacondas eat each other.

2566.   Rattlesnakes will never go out of their way to bite a human. However, people get regularly bitten by this snake because they are entranced by the sound its rattle makes. This snake bites more people than any other in the United States.

2567.   A snake's spine consists of between 200 to 400 vertebrae.

2568.   The Spider-Tailed Horned Viper in Western Iran is exactly what it sounds like; a snake with a tail that resembles a spider.

2569.   The venom from the Thailand Cobra is worth $152,835.82 per gallon, making it the most expensive liquid in the world.

2570.   Cats don't like long cylinder shapes (bananas, cucumbers, etc.) because felines are hard-wired to be scared of anything that resembles a snake.

2571.   The most venomous snakes are the Inland Taipan, the Eastern Brown Snake, the Coastal Taipan, the Tiger Snake, and the Black Tiger Snake.

2572.   The Inland Taipan has enough venom in its sac to kill 80 people.

2573.   Ireland is one of the only countries in the world not to have snakes. Ironically, snakes play an important role in Irish mythology.

2574.   Boas and pythons have little nubs, which shows that their ancestors use to have legs.

2575.   It takes weeks for a large snake to digest its prey.

2576.   The Anaconda is the heaviest snake, weight 595lbs.

2577.   Some snakes have up to 400 ribs. Humans only have 24.

2578.   Mongooses are immune to snake venom.

2579.   There are five kinds of "flying snakes" that can glide up to 330ft through the air.

2580.   Scales cover every part of a snake including its eyes.

2581.   The Gardener Snake is the most common snake in the US.

2582.   Some snakes don't have scales.

2583.   Snakes fangs fall out after two months.

2584.   The Arafura File Snake lays one egg every decade.

2585.   Snakes can eat between 6-30 meals a year.

2586.   The Mozambique Spitting Cobra can spit venom over 8ft away. It can do this with astonishing accuracy, even if it's lying on the ground.

2587.   The Gaboon Viper has the longest fangs of any

snake, measuring two inches long.

2588. Snakes use their tongue to smell.

2589. Anacondas can hold their breath for 10 minutes.

2590. Sea Snakes can dive 300ft under water.

2591. If a snake is threatened by a predator shortly after having a meal, it will regurgitate its food to make itself lighter so it can escape faster.

2592. The King Cobra is the smartest snake.

2593. The King Cobra is one of the few snakes that cares for its young. Most snakes abandon their younglings soon after their birth.

2594. The rattle of a rattlesnake is made of keratin; the same material that makes up human hair and fingernails.

2595. In 2009, an East African farm worker fought a 12ft python for three hours. Luckily, he survived.

2596. The Brazilian Pet Viper's venom is used to treat high blood pressure.

2597. Snakes can get so hot, that they fall into a summer version of hibernation known as aestivation.

2598. The word "cobra" means "hooded."

2599. The Black Mamba is the world's fastest snake. It can move at 12mph.

2600. Snakes never stop growing.

2601.   The snake is the most likely animal to be born with two heads. It's not uncommon for one of the snakes to try and eat the other.

2602.   Many non-venomous snakes are very helpful to humans since they kill pests and rodents like rats and mice.

2603.   The US Army Special Forces are taught how to safely kill and eat snakes during their training. They are known as Snake Eaters.

2604.   The first written record of snakes was in the Brooklyn Papyrus from Ancient Egypt in 450B.C.

2605.   Some snakes have three lungs.

2606.   Poisonous snakes have diamond-shaped pupils. Non-poisonous snakes have round pupils.

2607.   70% of snakes lay eggs. Those that lay eggs are called oviparous. The other 30% give birth to live young because they live in places that are too cold for an egg to hatch.

2608.   Venomous snakes can poison themselves to death.

2609.   If a snake gets too hot, it will become disoriented and might try to eat itself.

Spiders

2610. There are 46,000 types of spider. Only 12 species are dangerous to humans.

2611. Spiders kill 2,000 insects a year.

2612. A group of spiders is called a clutter.

2613. A baby spider is called a spiderling.

2614. Ok, the big question – What is the difference between a spider and a tarantula? Most people will say that spiders are bigger and furrier than normal spiders but it's more complicated than that. Tarantulas are part of the spider-family, Mygalomorphae. Tarantulas have fangs that point down while true spiders have pincer-like teeth.

   Tarantulas have retractable claws, don't spin webs, they can regenerate lost legs, and live for 30 years.

   Although they are usually hairy and large, some of them are very small and hairless.

2615. There are 900 species of tarantula.

2616. Giant tarantulas keep little frogs as pets to protect its eggs.

2617. Spiders eat their webs to recycle them.

2618. Some spiders can walk on water.

2619. NASA scientists gave drugs to spiders to see how it affected their webs.

   Spiders on marijuana wove half a web and then crawled away.

Spiders on caffeine chucked a few strands together.

Spiders on Benzedrine wove long webs with massive holes in-between the strands.

Spiders on LSD spun long lines without connecting them.

It was the most necessary scientific experiment in history.

2620.   95% of the spiders in the average house have never been outside.

2621.   Spiders can spin webs in zero gravity.

2622.   A spider's central nervous spills into its legs.

2623.   Arachnophobia is the fear of spiders. It is the most common fear in the world.

2624.   Spiders kill many insects that humans hate including flies, bees, and mosquitoes.

2625.   Spiders have a safety thread when they navigate through dangerously high places, similar to a rock climber. If they fall, their line will stop them from hitting the ground.

2626.   If a spider navigates itself downward to a new terrain, it will remain attached to its thread just in case it sees a predator and needs to hoist itself back up.

2627.   Some spiders kill tarantulas.

2628.   Many people assume that spiders have some special enzyme that makes them immune to sticking to their own webs. But they don't. Spiders only walk on their web with the tips of their legs. Falling into their own web will cause them to become stuck just like their prey.

2629.   Only two spiders in the US are dangerous; the Brown Recluse and the Black Widow.

2630.   Spiders will never go out of their way to bite a human and will almost never bite a person while they are asleep.

2631.   Nobody has died from a spider bite since 1981.

2632.   Certain spiders can breathe under water.

2633.   The Bird-Dropping Spider looks like bird feces. Because of this, birds don't attack it.

2634.   Spiders don't have genitalia.

2635.   Spiders can give birth to 3,000 eggs at a time.

2636.   The Wolf Spider carries her babies on her back.

2637.   A tarantula can liquefy the body of a mouse in two days.

2638.   The venom of a Black Widow is 15 times stronger than the venom of a rattlesnake.

2639.   Although the Black Widow has the reputation for being the most dangerous spider, the Brazilian Wandering Spider has the most powerful venom of all the arachnids.

2640.   Most spiders live for a year.

2641.   Some tarantulas can live over 20 years.

2642.   The Bola Spider uses a silk thread with a sticky droplet at the end. The droplet smells like a female moth, which attracts male moths. Once a moth comes in contact with the it, it sticks to the droplet, allowing the spider to devour it.

2643.   Silk webs contain vitamin K, which can stop bleeding wounds.

2644.   Spiders have been found on mountains that are 23,000ft high. Until these spiders were spotted, no one thought spiders could survive on elevated land of this magnitude.

2645.   Jumping Spiders can leap 40 times their own body length. This would be like a human jumping 230ft.

2646.   Surprisingly, a Jumping Spider doesn't have strong muscle legs. Instead, it contracts muscles in its abdomen, which forces liquid into its back legs. When its legs straighten, it catapults the spider forward.

2647.   Peacock Spiders dance to find a mate. No two peacock spiders have the same dance.

2648.   When a Wheel Spider is scared, it tucks its legs in and rolls away.

2649.   Trapdoor Spiders build trapdoors from soil and silk and lie in wait for their prey to walk by before leaping out and grabbing them.

2650.   50,000 spiders can live on a single web.

2651.   The world's biggest spider is the Goliath Birdeater. It weighs as much as a puppy and its legs are the length of a child's arm. It can live for 25 years and has fangs strong enough to pierce a human skull.

2652.   When people hear the word "web," they picture an orb web. However, spiders can use webs to make sheets, tangles, and ladders. Some spiders in Peru can even create web fences.

2653.   The Ray Spider uses its web as a slingshot to shoot its body at airborne prey.

2654.   The Bagheera Kiplingi is the only spider that is a herbivore.

2655.   Net-Throwing Spiders throw their web over their prey.

2656.   Most spiders create a new web every day.

2657.   No matter how many times a spider's web is destroyed, it will make another one.

2658.   The Gold Orb Weaver's web can last for years.

2659.   The US States Defense Department are trying to use Gold Orb Weaver silk to create bulletproof vests.

2660.   The Darwin Bark Spider creates the strongest material made by a living organism. Their webs are 10 times stronger than Kevlar armor.

2661.   Some webs are so strong, they can catch birds.

2662.   Some spiders can run 2ft per second.

2663.   Spiders are scared of ants.

2664.   Although the Black Widow has a reputation for

its venom, only the female is deadly.

2665.   The female Red Widow eats the male while they are mating. However, the male literally force-feeds himself to the female by putting his head in her mandibles. If she spits him out, he will repeatedly place himself back in until she devours him.

2666.   Some male spiders give dead flies to the females as a gift.

2667.   About a million spiders live in one acre of land in the Western world. About three million live in one acre in the tropics.

2668.   Spiders can zip-line on a line of silk. This is called ballooning.

2669.   In India, spiders' webs can cover trees for miles.

2670.   Some spiders can see UV light, which is invisible to humans.

2671.   Spiders are very important in maintaining a stable ecosystem. They pollinate plants and recycle dead animals and plants.

2672.   All spiders spin silk but not all spiders spin webs.

2673.   A female Black Widow only needs to mate once in its life.

2674.   Tarantulas can shoot hairs at predators, much like how a porcupine can fire its quills.

2675.   During the 16th and 17th century, Italians believed you wouldn't die from a venomous spider bite if you performed a dance. This inspired a dance called the tarantella.

2676.   Water Spiders use their legs as fishing poles to catch insects, tadpoles, and even fish.

2677.   Spiders don't have teeth. They inject digestive juices into the innards of their prey and then suck them up.

2678.   Most arachnophobes are more scared of tarantulas than spiders simply because they are bigger. However, the most venomous tarantula has a bite that's only as strong as a wasp sting.

2679.   When a spider is walking, it always has four legs on the ground and four legs in the air at any given moment.

2680.   The word "spider" is derived from the Old English word "spithra," which means "spinner."

2681.   Unlike most animals, spiders have muscles on the inside of their skeleton.

2682.   NASA have created robots for space designed to resemble spiders called Spidernauts that can crawl on the outside of a spacecraft and repair machinery.

2683.   The spider's silk is liquidated when its spewed out but it hardens almost instantly when it's exposed to the air.

2684.   Some spiders have up to seven different silk glands, each creating a different type of silk. Silk can be smooth, stick, dry, or stretchy.

2685.   If you put a spider outside, it usually dies within minutes because it has adapted to the heat of the building it was in.

2686.   Spiders can't stand the smell of a burnt chestnut.

2687.   Spider silk is five times stronger than steel in proportion to its weight. A spider's web as thick as a pencil could stop a jumbo jet in mid-flight. Scientists have no idea how to replicate the strength and elasticity of spider silk.

Squid

2688.   There are 304 species of squid.

2689.   Squid are mollusks that look like octopi except their heads are cylinder-shaped instead of spherical-shaped.

2690.   Squid have 10 tentacles; eight arms to grab prey or attack predators and two legs to project their body forward.

2691.   Their tentacles grow back if they get cut off.

2692.   The Big Fin Squid is the only squid that has 12 tentacles instead of 10.

2693.   Most squids only live for 1-2 years.

2694.   They have three hearts.

2695.   The squid's eye has more similarities to the human eye than any other animal.

2696.   The Humboldt Squid turns red to hide from predators. Red can't be seen well at the depth this squid lives in because the wavelength of light doesn't travel well.

2697.   The Colossal Squid is 46ft long and weighs 1,650lbs. It is the world's biggest mollusk and invertebrate and has the largest beak and eye in the animal kingdom. Its eye is 1ft wide.

2698.   Although the Colossal Squid was named in 1925, it wasn't seen until recently. In fact, many people believed it was a fictional animal. Many biologists speculated its existence for decades after seeing sucker-marks on a Sperm Whale that were the size of tractor tires.

2699.   They move with their tail in front.

2700.   The Giant Squid's brain is shaped like a doughnut.

2701.   Some squid have bioluminescent organs, which makes them glow in the dark.

2702.   Most biologists believe that there could be 200 species of squid yet to be identified.

2703.   The most terrifying cephalopod has to be the Vampire Squid. This creature has red eyes, black skin, and webbed tentacles.

2704.   Under a microscope, a squid's tentacles look like hundreds of Venus Flytraps.

2705.   Its large head is called a mantle.

2706.   Like octopi, squid squirt ink. Their ink contains dopamine, which triggers the pleasure part of the brain. If a person gets exposed to this ink, they will get a buzz similar to the drug, MDMA.

2707.   The Heteroteuthis Dispar shoots bioluminescent mucus from its ink sacs. When it fights predators, it looks like its shooting light.

2708.   Squids are so similar to cuttlefish, that the Spanish language doesn't have a word to differentiate the two. Even marine biologists have difficulty distinguishing the creatures without dissecting them.

<u>Squirrels</u>

2709.   Squirrels are rodents that belong to the Sciuridae family.

2710.   Squirrels can't see the color red.

2711.   Squirrels have been around for 35 million years.

2712.   There are 285 species of squirrels.

2713.   "Squirrel" means "shadow-tailed oak."

2714.   Squirrels breed twice a year.

2715.   They eat nuts, insects, eggs, birds, and snakes.

2716.   The biggest squirrel is the Indian Giant Squirrel, which measures 3ft in length.

2717.   The Flying Squirrel has a furry membrane called a patagia between its wrists and ankles. The patagia works like a built-in kite that allows the squirrel to glide up to 295ft.

2718.   A group of squirrels is called a dray or a scurry.

2719.   Squirrels bury their nuts in special places, hoping no predators will find their food. They actually make fake food burials to trick potential thieves while the real food is hidden elsewhere.

Starfish

2720.   Starfish don't have brains.

2721.   If you cut a starfish in half, the two pieces will turn into two starfish. In fact, a single arm can regenerate an entire body.

2722.   Starfish have filtered seawater instead of blood.

2723.   Starfish are the only animals that turn their stomach inside out.

2724.   The xyloplax is the only starfish that lives off trees.

2725.   There is a starfish with a human-looking mouth.

2726.   Starfish have eyes at the end of each arm.

2727.   Starfish used to be known as sea stars.

2728.   There are 2,000 types of starfish.

2729.   Some starfish have up to 40 arms.

Swans

2730.   A group of swans is called a lamentation. When a group of swans is in captivity, it is called a fleet.

2731.   A male swan is called a cob. A female swan is called a pen.

2732.   Black swans are native to Australia.

2733.   A baby swan is called a cygnet or a flapper.

2734.   Swans can fly 60mph.

2735.   Swans are the largest birds that can fly.

2736.   A fear of swans is called kiknophobia.

2737.   Swans are strong enough to break a person's arm.

2738.   Swans can remember human faces and will hold grudges against people who are mean to them.

2739.   The Whistling Swan has 25,000 feathers.

2740.   There are six species of swan.

Tigers

2741. There are more Siberian tigers in captivity than in the wild.

2742. Tigers are the only predators to prey on adult bears.

2743. There are more tigers in the US than every other country combined.

2744. Many white tigers are cross-eyed.

2745. Tigers became extinct in Cambodia in 2016.

2746. A baby tiger is called a cub or a whelp.

2747. A group of tigers is called a streak.

2748. Tigers have striped skin as well as striped fur.

2749. No two tigers have the same stripe pattern.

2750. 95.6% of a housecat's DNA is identical to a tiger's.

2751. A tiger's tongue is so coarse, it could lick a human's flesh down to the bone.

2752. The largest cat in the world is a liger, which is a crossbreed between a male lion and a female tiger. Because of a genetic abnormality, ligers suffer from dysplasia, which means they never stop growing. Although a tiger can weigh 600lbs, a liger can be as heavy over 1,000lbs.

2753. Bengal tigers attack 60 people per year in the Ganges Delta. When the inhabitants realized that tigers didn't attack humans when they are facing them, people started wearing masks on the back of their heads. Amazingly, tiger attacks went down.

2754.   There are no tigers in Africa.

2755.   Mike Tyson owns a pet tiger.

2756.   Poachers use the code words "striped t-shirt" when referring to a tiger or tiger skin.

2757.   Tigers only roar at each other.

Toads

2758.   Okay. What is the difference between a frog and a toad?

Well, a frog has smooth, clammy skin, while toads have dry, bumpy skin.

Also, toads spend more time on land than frogs and have shorter legs.

2759.   A group of toads is called a knot. A group of toad eggs are called a clutch.

2760.   When a tadpole turns into a toad, it is known as a toadlet.

2761.   Toad tadpoles have larger, blacker heads than frog tadpoles. Toad tadpoles also have shorter tails.

2762.   The most common toad is the European Toad.

2763.   Females are larger than males.

2764.   Toads don't jump like frogs. They crawl at 5mph.

2765.   The Cane Toad was introduced to Australia to combat the beetles from destroying the sugarcane plantations. However, the Cane Toad has now become a widespread pest to the country.

2766.   If a toad feels stressed, it will excrete a poison from a pair of parotoid glands on the back of its head.

2767.   Toads sometimes play dead when they are confronted with a large predator.

2768.   Toads are nocturnal.

2769. They can live up to 50 years.

2770. A toad can lay 1,500-5,000 eggs in one go.

2771. Their predators are foxes, snakes, and hedgehogs.

2772. They eat earwigs, spiders, insects, worms, and snails.

2773. Although most toads are brown, they can be green, yellow, or black.

2774. Female toads don't make sounds.

Tortoises

2775.   Differentiating a tortoise from a turtle is pretty simple. A tortoise has four normal legs and is unable to swim. A turtle's can easily swim and their front legs are fin-shaped.

2776.   The Desert Tortoise is a fascinating reptile. When it eats plants, it eats the entire thing, whether it be an herb, shrub, or a cactus. Since it eats every part of a plant, they excrete a lot of fertilized waste because they've absorbed so many seeds. This process allows the tortoise to sustain itself and other life within the desert. This gives the desert tortoise the nickname of "the accidental gardener."

2777.   A group of tortoises is called a creep.

2778.   The tortoise's shell is not just armor; it is a part of the tortoise. The reptile will be hurt if its shell is damaged.

2779.   A new type of tortoise was discovered on the Galapagos Islands in 2015, even though the extremely slow reptile was nipping about the small island for over a century. Somehow, it took 100 years for someone to notice it. It is called the Chelonoidis Donfaustoi Tortoise.

2780.   Charles Darwin's pet tortoise, Harriet, lived to be 176. When Darwin died, the tortoise was looked after by Steve Irwin.

2781.   The scales on its body are called scutes. They are made of keratin, which is the same material that makes hair and fingernails.

2782.   A tortoise's shell becomes brighter in hot areas.

2783.   Although tortoises can't swim, they can hold their breath for a long time.

2784.   Its shell is made of 60 bones.

2785.   They eat grass, ferns, fruits, flowers, and tree leaves.

2786.   Females lay 1-30 eggs at once.

2787.   The female is usually larger than the male.

2788.   Tortoises are the oldest land animals in the world.

2789.   The oldest tortoise ever is Jonathan. He was born in 1832 and is currently still alive at the age of 184.

2790.   They smell with their throats.

2791.   Leonardo DiCaprio has a pet tortoise.

2792.   Tortoises can breed and lay eggs until the day they die.

2793.   Female Galapagos Giant tortoises find long-necked tortoises attractive.

2794.   During sieges, the Roman military would get into testudo formation, which means that the soldiers would put shields in front of them and above their heads, so they resembled a walking shell. The soldiers came up with this strategy by observing tortoises. Even the name, "tetsudo" means "tortoise."

2795.   The reason tortoises move so slowly is because they evolved so they never needed to rely on speed. They mostly eat plants which don't move. They don't need to run away from predators since they can hide in their shell. They can survive for a very long time without eating so they don't need to rush to their next meal. Also, their shell is very heavy so they can't move very fast even if they wanted to.

2796.   Many people assume that tortoises age like a human, but at a much slower rate. But it's much stranger than that. When a tortoise reaches its 40s or 50s, it will become sexually mature. At this point, the tortoise does something very odd. It stops aging for almost a century. Geneticists have great difficulty finding out how old tortoises are because there might be no genetic difference between a 55-year-old tortoise and a 95-year-old tortoise.

Once it reaches 100 years or so, it will then resume aging.

<u>Tuataras</u>

2797.   The tuatara is hands-down the weirdest reptile in the world. In fact, it's not really a reptile. Many scientists would consider it a proto-reptile, since it has many features that no other reptile on Earth has.

2798.   Although it seems to have a double row of teeth, it's been recently discovered that the tuatara doesn't have teeth at all. Instead, it has teeth-shaped protrusions extending from its jaws.

2799.   The tuatara has a third eye. Although many reptiles and amphibians have a third parietal eye like frogs, lizards, and salamanders, the tuatara's third eye is fully developed and possesses its own lens, cornea, retina, and rod-like cells just like its two other eyes.

2800.   Tuataras live for over a century.

2801.   Tuataras breed once every 2-5 years.

2802.   Tuataras are worshipped by the Maori tribe.

2803.   They can stay fertile for an incredibly long time. One tuatara became a father when he was 111.

2804.   Tuataras invade bird's nests and live there. They are one of the few animals in the animal kingdom that break into the home of another animal but live peacefully. They rarely harm the mother bird or her chicks and will actually defend them against other predators.

2805.   These animals can be found on 32 islands in New Zealand.

2806.   It's directly related to the first known reptile, Hylonomus lyelli.

2807.   Unlike other reptiles, it has feathers, although they are very difficult to see.

2808.   It is the only modern reptile to have a beak-like jaw.

2809.   It has the most primitive hearing of any amniote (egg-laying animal.) The fact that it's still alive after over 200 million years considering its practically deaf is staggering.

2810.   The strangest thing about tuataras is that they are the fastest evolving creature to date. Although they look like they haven't changed their appearance in millions of years, they are the only creatures on Earth that are evolving on a molecular level! Although its physical appearance hasn't changed in 200 million years, its DNA, RNA, and proteins have dramatically changed over the last 8,000 years.

Turkeys

2811. Many people don't know that turkeys can fly. Wild turkeys can fly up to 55mph.

2812. Turkeys originated from Mexico.

2813. A group of turkeys is called a rafter.

2814. A baby turkey is called a poult.

2815. A male turkey is called a jake, a tom, or a gobbler. A female turkey is called a hen.

2816. Gobblers have hair-like bristles that grow from their chest. These bristles resemble a beard and a gobbler can have up to eight of them.

2817. Some people snap a turkey's wishbone in two to bring good fortune. This bone is called a furcular.

2818. Wild turkeys sleep in trees.

2819. Turkeys have periscopic vision so it can see objects that are not in its direct line of vision. It can rotate its head so it has a 360-degree field of vision.

2820. The long flap of flesh that hangs over a turkey's beak is called a snood.

2821. The red skin that hangs from its neck is called a wattle.

2822. The fleshy bumps on the top of its head is called a caruncle.

2823. Hens don't gobble. Only gobblers do. Instead, hens

cluck and chirp.

2824. Their predators are foxes, raccoons, and coyotes.

2825. 45 million turkeys are eaten in the US during Thanksgiving.

Turtles

2826.   Turtles dig rain basins. They will carve out a section of sand to collect water when it rains. When it becomes too hot, the turtle will seek refuge in the hole and drink the water to stay hydrated.

2827.   Hawksbill Sea Turtles eat toxic sponges. These turtles can eat so many of these sponges, that humans can die from secondary poisoning after eating the turtle.

2828.   Male turtles grunt. Females hiss.

2829.   A group of turtles is called a bale.

2830.   Turtles can eat glass and not be harmed by it. Scientists have no idea how they accomplish this.

2831.   Some turtles are strong enough to kill ducks.

2832.   Turtles have existed for 120 million years.

2833.   When a turtle gets tired swimming, it sometimes hitches a ride on top of a crocodile.

2834.   Approximately 50 million years ago, there were turtles that were bigger than a car that ate crocodiles.

2835.   The Hawkbill Turtle is the only reptile that glows.

2836.   The Chinese Soft-Shelled Turtle is the only animal that urinates through its mouth.

2837.   It's illegal to sit on a sea turtle in the US.

2838.   The Leatherback turtles travel 22mph underwater, making them the fastest turtles.

2839.   Certain turtles use a stink gland as a defense
mechanism, much like a skunk.

Vultures

2840. Vultures eat 70% of all the dead meat in Africa.

2841. Although vultures are immune to most diseases like rabies, anthrax, salmonella, and cholera, they are not resistant to all insects. This can be a problem since they come into contact with flies and parasites while they feast on rotting carcasses. To counter this, vultures urinate on their bodies while eating to remove any potential infectants from parasites.

2842. A vulture has no feathers on its head or neck. This is to prevent bacteria and parasites from burrowing into its feathers, which could cause infections on its face.

2843. Many farmers loathe vultures, believing that the birds prey on their livestock. Although it's true that vultures occasionally attack living prey, it's only when the animal is very feeble or dying and wouldn't be much use to the farmer.

2844. The Andean Condor has the largest wingspan of any vulture, measuring 11ft wide.

2845. They have weak legs and feet but very strong bills, which allows them to penetrate a carcass with little effort.

2846. The Palm-Nut Vulture is the only one of its kind that is a vegetarian.

2847. If a vulture sees a dead animal in water, it will try to drag it out onto dry land. This indirectly stops water from being polluted in Africa.

2848.   There are 23 species of vultures. 14 species are endangered.

2849.   The Griffin Vulture flies 6.8 miles high, which is higher than any other bird.

2850.   Vultures live on every continent except Antarctica and Australia.

2851.   A group of vulture is called a volt. When vultures are in flight, they are known as a kettle. A group of vultures feeding together is called a wake.

2852.   They have an excellent sense of sight and smell, which they rely on to locate food.

2853.   They usually eat the eyes of their prey first because they are easy to pierce open.

2854.   Contrary to what many cartoons show, vultures don't circle dying animals.

2855.   Vultures are carnivorous and almost exclusively eat rotting meat. Although they prefer fresh meat, they usually wait until the carcass is so rotting, that no animal would go near it. Vultures do this to avoid the risk of being attacked while eating.

Walruses

2856.   This arctic marine mammal has flippers, a broad head, a short muzzle, small eyes, whiskers, and large tusks.

2857.   There are two subspecies of walrus – the Atlantic walrus and the Pacific walrus.

2858.   Walruses are cinnamon colored.

2859.   According to J.R.R. Tolkien (who wrote The Lord of the Rings,) the word "walrus" is derived from the Dutch word "walvis," which means "whale."

2860.   Their hind flippers can be turned forward to help them move on land.

2861.   Their front flippers have five digits.

2862.   They use their tusks to defend themselves, cut through ice, and get out of water.

2863.   A male walrus' tusks are usually one-meter-long and weigh 12lbs each.

2864.   They measure about 10ft long and 6ft tall.

2865.   Walruses weigh up to 4,400lbs.

2866.   Its skin weighs 1,100lbs.

2867.   A group of walruses is called a herd.

2868.   Walruses have 450 whiskers called vibrissae.

2869.   Walruses have 400-700 vibrissae in 14 rows

reach 12 inches in length.

2870.   Although both male and female walruses have tusks, the males are bigger.

2871.   The tusks never stop growing.

2872.   They can dive 260ft into the ocean.

2873.   They can hold their breath for 30 minutes.

2874.   To prevent oxygen loss underwater, they store oxygen in their blood and muscles when they dive. Because of this, they have two or three times more blood than any land mammal of their size.

2875.   Walruses are covered in blubber, which helps insulate themselves from the cold.

2876.   The scientific name for a walrus is Odobenus rosmarus, which is Latin for "tooth-walking sea-horse."

2877.   They eat clams, mussels, and dead seals.

2878.   It is illegal to hunt walruses.

2879.   There are 250,000 walruses in the world. 200,000 of them are Pacific walruses.

2880.   Walruses live in Canada and Greenland.

2881.   They spend 66% of their lives in water.

2882.   The sound effect for the T-Rex in the film, Jurassic Park, was actually a walrus' roar.

<u>Wasps</u>

2883.   Bone-House Wasps are so-called because they make their home from the bodies of their prey.

2884.   The venom in wasps contains a pheromone that causes other wasps to become more aggressive. If you swat a wasp, it'll release this pheromone, alerting all of its buddies to attack you.

2885.   When a wasp stings you, it can hurt for about 24 hours. However, a small number of people who are stung will suffer an anaphylactic shock, which can be fatal.

2886.   A wasp sting can be treated with any deodorant that contains aluminum.

2887.   Although bees swarm, wasps don't.

2888.   There is a wasp that lays its eggs in cockroaches. The eggs will produce a neurotoxin that will control the cockroach's mind. All the wasp has to do is tug on the cockroach's antennae to direct it forward.
     When the wasp's egg eventually hatches, the larvae burst through the cockroach and then gorge on the body.
     Although this isn't the only form of mind control in the animal kingdom, it's certainly the creepiest.
     And because this wasp leaves its prey into a husk of its former self, it is known as the Dementor Wasp; named after the creatures in Harry Potter that steal the lifeforce from their victims.

Whales

2889.   Whales belong to the cetacean order, which means they are mammals that have adapted to aquatic life.

2890.   There are two suborders of whales; toothed whales and baleen whales. Sperm Whales and Beluga Whales are toothed whales and prey on large fish. Baleen whales include Blue Whales and Humpback Whales and eat thousands of small creatures like krill and plankton. Instead of teeth, baleen whales have a comb-like structure in their mouth called a baleen that filters in small creatures but keeps out larger fish that the whale can't digest.

2891.   Humpback Whales let dolphins hitch rides on their head for fun.

2892.   Whales have accents.

2893.   Whales name each other.

2894.   Sperm Whales have no upper teeth.

2895.   A Beluga Whale called Noc lived in captivity for 30 years in San Diego. One day, Noc did something extremely unusual. Anytime a diver entered his tank, Noc would get visibly upset and make a noise that sounded like, "Out" as if he wanted the diver to get out of his tank. Once the diver left Noc alone, he would stop making this noise.

   Now, any rational person would think that the whale wasn't actually speaking English but making a sound that coincidentally sounded like "Out." This isn't uncommon. Cats often make sounds that resemble human speech.

But it's not that simple. In order for Noc to make this sound, he spoke several octaves lower than any Beluga whale ever has in history. He was going out of his way to make this sound to show his irritation.

2896.   A Blue Whale's heart is the size of a car.

2897.   There's only one white Humpback Whale in the world.

2898.   About 100 whales are killed by humans every day.

2899.   Narwhal Whales are known as "the whale with a horn on its head." However, the horn is actually a tooth. It starts in the Narwhal's mouth but then pierces through its skull. This is known as an "erupted tooth." It is super-sensitive because it has millions of nerve-endings, which helps the whale tell the difference between fresh water and salt water. These whales can only live in salt water so the tooth is evolution's way of keeping it alive.

2900.   When people saw a narwhal's skeleton many centuries ago, they believed it to be a horned horse.
          That's right. It was the narwhal that inspired the unicorn myth, not the horse.

2901.   Whales can only hold their breath for 30 minutes.

2902.   Whales' ancestors used to live on land. For reasons unknown, they went back into the sea.

2903.   Whales have ankles.

2904.   Despite a Blue Whale's size, they only eat krill, a shrimp-like animal about the size of a peanut.

2905. A Blue Whale's heart beats 25 times per minute.

2906. Blue Whales can get a tan.

2907. Sperm Whales sleep vertically.

2908. During the 18th and 19th century, whales were hunted for their oil, which was used for lamps.

2909. Baby Blue Whales gain 200lbs a day.

2910. Humans have been hunting whales since the Stone Age.

2911. The water in a Blue Whale's mouth weighs as much as its entire body.

2912. Many perfumes are made from whale organs.

2913. Whales suffer from sunburn.

2914. A new whale called the Omura's Whale was discovered in 2015. It is one of the smallest whales, measuring 34ft.

2915. The Bowhead Whale can live for 200 years, making it the oldest living mammal.

2916. Sperm Whales can dive two miles deep

2917. The Sperm Whale has the largest brain in the world, measuring 46lbs. By comparison, a human brain weighs 3lbs.

2918. "Whale" means "wheel."

2919.   Of the 11 baleen whales that exist, nine of them are endangered.

2920.   In recent years, researchers have learned about the depths of the ocean through submarines. Before this time, the only source of knowledge about the ocean's depths came from examining the contents of a Sperm Whale's stomach.

2921.   When a whale lifts its tail out of the water, it's called fluking.

2922.   When a whale jumps out of the water, it's called breaching. The Humpback Whale breaches more than any other whale. Scientists don't know why whales leap out of the water.

2923.   Baleen whales use sonar to communicate to each other.

2924.   A Sperm Whales is so-called because its forehead contains spermaceti, which can make up to 500 gallons of oil.

2925.   Whales have no natural predators apart from humans.

2926.   Moby Dick is based on a real murdering whale called Mocha Dick. The story of Mocha was depicted in the 2015 film, In the Heart of the Sea.

2927.   The Blue Whale is the largest animal that has ever existed. It is over twice as long as a Brachiosaurus. It weighs 173 tons. That's more than 34 African Elephants. It measures 107ft, which is longer than a basketball court.

2928.   Despite a Blue Whale's size, its throat is only the size of a beach ball.

2929.   Whales move their tails up and down, compared to fish who move their tails side to side.

2930.   Whales have existed for 50 million years.

2931.   Whale milk is 50% fat.

2932.   When a Blue Whale dives into the water, its head is already deeper than most scuba divers go before its tail leaves the surface of the water.

2933.   In 2007, a Bowhead Whale was discovered with a harpoon in its neck. The harpoon had stopped being manufactured in 1890, meaning the whale was carrying it for over a century.

Wolves

2934. Wolf drawings have been found in caves in southern Europe that date back to 20,000B.C.

2935. When howling, no two wolves will howl on the same note to create the illusion that there are more wolves than there actually are.

2936. Wolves belong to the Canidae family (dogs, coyotes, dingos, jackals, foxes, etc.) Wolves are the largest members of the Canidae.

2937. Vikings wore wolf skins and drank their blood.

2938. Wolves run on their toes.

2939. They can smell other animals from a mile away.

2940. Most wolves are monogamous.

2941. Wolves can hear up to 10 miles away.

2942. Wolves used to be the most widely distributed land predator in the world.

2943. A wolf can eat 20lbs of meat in a single meal.

2944. A wolf pack usually contains two or three members but can have as many as 10.

2945. There are two main species of wolves; grey wolves and red wolves.

2946. There are 38 subspecies of Grey Wolf including Timber Wolves, Lobos, Buffalo Wolves, Arctic Wolves, and Tundra Wolves.

2947.   Red Wolves are different from Grey Wolves because they are smaller, have longer legs, and shorter fur.

2948.   Its jaw has a crushing pressure of 1,500lbs per square inch. That's twice as strong as a large dog.

2949.   There were two million Grey Wolves in the US in the 17th century. Nowadays, there are 65,000 in the US and only 150,000 worldwide.

2950.   Most female wolves will never have pups. The alpha wolf will mate with who he desires and the other female wolves will babysit his cubs.

2951.   Male wolves can become so intimidated by the alpha, they will not mate and suffer from a disorder called "psychological castration."

2952.   Wolves evolved from the Mesocyon. This dog-like creature lived 35 million years ago.

2953.   Wolves can swim for eight miles.

2954.   Adolf Hitler's first name means "Lead Wolf." If he had to give a fake name, he would usually call himself Commander Wolf. Some of his headquarters were called Werewolf, Wolf's Gulch, and Wolf's Lair.

2955.   In the 1600s, Ireland was known as Wolfland.

2956.   Wolves will respond to humans imitating their howls.

2957.   A wolf's eyes glow in the dark.

2958.   Wolves can drastically alter the ecosystem and geography of the land they live in. When they were introduced into Yellowstone National Park in 1995, trees grew faster and rivers changed their behavior due to new vegetation reducing erosion.

2959.   In 1927, a French policeman shot her boy because she was convinced he was a werewolf. That same year, all of the remaining wild wolves were killed.

2960.   The Dire Wolves in the television show, Game of Thrones, existed two million years ago. They used to hunt woolly mammoths.

2961.   Wolves usually trot at 5mph. They can run 20mph easily and when desperate, they can gallop 40mph for about two minutes.

2962.   The smallest wolves weigh 30lbs. They live in the Middle East.

2963.   The largest wolves weigh 175lbs and can be found in Canada, Alaska, and Russia.

2964.   Wolves will hunt at night and not just when there's a full Moon.

2965.   Ravens often follow wolves to eat the leftovers of whatever the wolves kill.

2966.   The Roman philosopher, Pliny the Elder, believed wolf teeth could be rubbed on the gums of babies to make teething less painless.

2967.   Wolves don't make good guard dogs because they are scared of others when they are alone. They only attack when they are in a pack.

2968.   Aztecs ate wolf liver to cure depression.

2969.   In the Middle Ages, Europeans used powdered wolf liver to ease the pain of childbirth.

2970.   Wolves went extinct in England in 1500.

2971.   Wolves went extinct in Ireland in 1770.

2972.   In 1934, Germany became the first country to place the wolf under protection.
        They were also the first animals to be put on the US Endangered Species Act list in 1973.

2973.   The Ancient Greeks believed that you would turn into a vampire if you ate a lamb that had been killed by a wolf.

2974.   Wolves use facial expressions to communicate.

2975.   The Japanese word for wolf translates into "great God."

2976.   During the 1600s, hundreds of people in Europe were killed for being suspected werewolves.

2977.   When a female wolf is threatened while she is near the father of her cubs, she will appear to hide under his neck. However, she is actually covering his throat from the assailant.

Woodpeckers

2978.   When a woodpecker's beak hits a tree, it's head is subject to 1,000 times the force of gravity.

2979.   They can peck 20 times per second.

2980.   Woodpeckers peck up to 12,000 times a day.

2981.   When a woodpecker drills into a tree, other birds can tell which bird it is based on the rhythm. It's like the bird version of a signature.

2982.   There are 180 species of woodpeckers.

2983.   The Gila Woodpeckers mainly live off cacti.

2984.   A woodpecker's tongue is 4 inches long. In some species, the tongue wraps around the inside of the skull when it is retracted.

Worms

2985.   It was only discovered in 2015 that worms use the magnetic field of the Earth to know where to move and where to find fresh soil.

2986.   There are 2,700 species of worms.

2987.   Scientists hope that to replicate a human brain and put it in a machine. So far, this has only been accomplished with one animal – the earthworm. It is currently inside of a Lego robot (I swear I'm not making this up.) This experiment is known as the OpenWorm project.

2988.   Worms eat their own droppings.

2989.   The deepest living animal is the Devil Worm, which lives 2.2 miles below the Earth's surface.

2990.   One acre of fertile land contains up to one million worms.

2991.   Worms are hermaphrodites since they have male and female organs.

2992.   Worms breathe through their skin since they have no lungs.

2993.   The Bobbit Worm is venomous and hunts by hiding in the ocean floor and snapping its jaws when its prey comes near. Its snap is so powerful, that it tends to cut fish in half. Also, this worm is 10ft long.

Zebras

2994.   Zebras injure more zookeepers in the US than any other animal.

2995.   Most people think zebras are white with black stripes. In reality, it's the other way around.

2996.   Zebras and ostriches often live together in the wild to protect each other from predators. The ostrich can see better and the zebra can hear and smell when danger is near.
    Also, the zebra has the strongest kick in the animal kingdom. The ostrich has the second strongest.

2997.   People briefly tried to domesticate the zebra but the animal proved too violent.

2998.   There are three kinds of zebra – the Plains Zebra, the Mountain Zebra, and the Grevy's Zebra.

2999.   A group of zebras is called a cohort, a dazzle, or a zeal.

3000.   Scientists have a scanner that can allow them to tell the difference between different zebras. The machine works exactly the same as a barcode scanner.

#0063 - 091116 - C0 - 175/108/17 - PB - DID1645343